# Thank God it's Monday

# Thank God it's Monday

## STRATEGIES FOR INCREASING JOB SATISFACTION

Charles Cameron and Suzanne Elusorr

Ebury Press London

Published by
Ebury Press
Division of the National
Magazine Company Ltd
Colquhoun House
27-37 Broadwick Street
London W1V 1FR

First impression 1986
Published in the United States of America
by Jeremy P Tarcher Inc.

ISBN 0 85223 579 8

Design by Dubé/Todd
Cover Design by Frank Phillips
Printed in Great Britain by The Bath Press, Bath

To Kenneth Cowan,
Job Company colleague and friend.

# ACKNOWLEDGMENTS

No book is ever written without considerable behind-the-scenes support from an author's colleagues, family, and friends. Our grateful thanks go to all those with whom we discussed this book during its evolution, and particularly to Mitchell Ditkoff, Peggy Hope, John Messer, Nancy O'Donohue, and William Ross, who read portions of the book while it was still in manuscript. We would also like to thank our editor, Laura Golden, who gave us courage when the sky was falling, and our indefatigable publisher, Jeremy Tarcher, whose personal vision and close editorial oversight contributed much to the final text.

# *Contents*

# Chapter 1

## WORK—AN AFFAIR OF THE HEART

*I didn't want to work. It was as simple as that.*
*I distrusted work, disliked it. I thought it was a*
*very bad thing that the human race had unfortu-*
*nately invented for itself.*

*Agatha Christie*

William Faulkner once remarked, "You can't eat for eight hours a day nor drink for eight hours a day nor make love for eight hours a day—all you can do for eight hours is work." Work occupies more of your time than almost anything else. In fact, it occupies so much of your waking life that job satisfaction isn't just a nice idea—if your life is to be fulfilling, it's essential.

Whether you are a young professional on your way up, a mother returning to the work force, a self-made millionaire looking for a renewed sense of purpose, a student preparing for a job interview, or someone who is considering changing careers, job satisfaction is one luxury you can't afford to be without.

Therefore:

— This book is about finding meaning in life—by finding it in the work you do.

— It is about shooting for the top—both in terms of satisfaction, and success.

— It is about increasing the level to which your work reflects your dreams, your delights and your ideals.

Most people devote forty hours a week, fifty weeks a year to work: so one year's work is an investment of 2,000 hours of your life. How much is your time worth per hour? Multiply that by 2,000, and then by the number of years you expect to work. That's roughly what the rest of your working life is worth to you in dollars. Now, how much time and effort do you feel should be put into researching and evaluating that kind of multithousand dollar investment? This will give you a picture of the amount of care that should go into the process of choosing the work you do.

It's a human life you are investing. Your own. You deserve a good return on your investment.

## WORK: PENITENTIARY OR PARADISE?

There are days when work is a hard grind, and days when it's a breeze. "I love the challenge," you say one day, and the next, "It's only a job." There are few things more exciting than getting a new job. But then the excitement wears off and the routine sets in, sometimes within the first month, week, or even day at work.

Thinking about work often brings both a sense of excitement and possibility, and a feeling of betrayal and frustration. Most people take the good with the bad and have a fairly balanced view of the whole affair: "Every job has its drawbacks, but this one is okay." Some people feel overwhelmingly good about their work, most of the time. They've found the kind of work that suits them well, and a few even admit they'd give money to be allowed to do the things they get paid to do.

But when people get stuck for a long time with a job that simply doesn't suit them, even when the pay is pretty decent, life can get really unpleasant. They want to say, in the words of a recent song, "You can take this job and shove it."

Just how many people are cursing under their breath as they drive to work every day? How many people, having spent the morning cooped up in an office, and then gone out to lunch on a beautiful day, have wondered as they got back into the car, "What if I don't go back? What if I just keep driving?"

The statistics on job satisfaction sometimes sound pretty optimistic. In 1982, 69 percent of Americans questioned in a Gallup poll stated that "having an interesting and enjoyable job" was "very important" to them, and 64 percent indicated that they were "highly satisfied" with the work they did.

On the other hand Studs Terkel, who knows his away around the American job scene as few others do, began the introduction to his book, *Working*, with these words: "This book, being about work, is, by its very nature, about violence —to the spirit as well as to the body. . . ." That's hardly the most optimistic opening.

It seems that when polled, most people put a good face on things, and see their jobs "in the best possible light"—but that when they are questioned in depth about their work by a writer as probing as Studs Terkel, a very different picture emerges.

Terkel is not simply picking up on a pervasive willingness to let off steam, grumble and complain. A sixteen-year study of 350,000 job applicants conducted at the California State University, Fullerton, concluded that 80 percent of the people they interviewed felt they were in the wrong jobs.

A recent University of Michigan study found that more than one out of every four American workers felt so ashamed of the quality of the products they were producing that they themselves would not want to buy them. People who wouldn't want to use what they make probably don't receive very much satisfaction in making it.

Elliot Liebow, director of the Center for Work and Mental Health at the National Institute of Mental Health, wrote that "the way work is defined in our society, the way in which it's organized, structured, rewarded, and withheld, is one of the main generators of social and mental health problems."

What's wrong? Why do so many people find their work less than rewarding, less than satisfactory? If five to six is the "happy hour," what's going on from nine to five? Or to put it another way, why has "Thank God it's Friday" come to be a catch phrase, a popular bumper sticker, and even the name of a chain of restaurants?

Terkel puts his finger on what many people are missing in their work when he characterizes the job search as a quest for "daily meaning as well as daily bread, for recognition as well as cash, for astonishment rather than torpor; in short, for a sort of life rather than a Monday-through-Friday sort of dying. Perhaps immortality, too, is part of the quest."

Meaning. Recognition. Astonishment. What might work that includes these ingredients be like? Are there ways to bring these qualities into whatever work we are already doing? How can we find work that contains more of these qualities?

## THE ULTIMATE SEDUCTION

People who really enjoy their work, who find that it offers them real satisfaction and that elusive hint of "immortality," declare that work can be one of the headiest, strongest love affairs in the world. It feels terrific, they say. Even when it's demanding, it's utterly rewarding. Picasso expressed it like this: "It is your work in life that is the ultimate seduction." This book is about finding "your work in life," not just having a job that gets you by.

When the well-known British economist E.F. Schumacher wrote his book *Small Is Beautiful,* he subtitled it "Economics as if People Mattered." This book is dedicated to the proposition that real work is work with meaning: "work as if people mattered." *TGIM\** is therefore based on two seemingly very simple principles:

— Love the work you do.

— Do the work you love.

The first principle can be applied even in situations where financial considerations leave you no choice about the work you must do. Finding ways to love a job that you presently hate is not an easy business, but it is not necessarily impossible.

The second principle advises you about what work to choose if you have a choice. And, as this book may help you discover, you probably have more choices than you think.

Very few jobs are so terrible that you'd need to rely entirely on the first principle to enjoy them, and jobs that are so wonderful that you can rely entirely on the second are even more rare. As a result, you probably need to approach the issue of work satisfaction from both ends—using some strategies to bring your work more closely in line with your passions and your loves, and others to cope with the less satisfying areas that almost every job includes.

This book suggests broad strategies and specific tactics for implementing both principles. It offers ways in which even a seemingly boring and routine job can be made fascinating, and provides you with tools for investigating your passions, values, and beliefs to discover the work you'd love.

## AN OVERVIEW OF THE BOOK

This is a book of commonsense ideas that we tend to forget under the pressures of money, success, the boss, and our bills. The following brief overview is intended to let you know what you are signing up for.

The first section explores your current work and suggests that there are three major levels of work satisfaction. First, you work to make a living, to pay your way in the world; your work can and should give you financial satisfaction. Second, your work can involve the pursuit and fulfilment of your interests, and serve as a vehicle for self-expression; it can give you personal satisfaction. Third, your work can be a vehicle for making a contribution to the world around you; it is this, in the long run, which can bring you the deepest satisfaction.

Section Two proposes five strategies for increasing the degree to which one's work includes a balance of these three kinds of satisfaction. These five strategies are offered in what is roughly an ascending scale, from making the best of a less-than-perfect situation, to finding optimal work.

— "Zenning It" offers you a strategy by which almost any work circumstance, however unfavorable, can be turned to your advantage. It suggests some ways of dealing with the boredom and frustration so common in the workplace.

— "Underwriting Your True Work" describes the option of working one's "official" job as a means of financing one's "true work," which is then conducted in one's spare time. It also discusses the pitfalls of this approach, and how to avoid them.

— "Learning and Changing" is another option we discuss. Turning your work into a "school for life" brings satisfaction in its own right. It enhances your marketable skills, and it is the key to survival in a rapidly changing world.

— "The Inside Job" offers a strategy whereby you work at a "cover" job in accordance with an "official" job description, while obtaining your satisfaction from the simultaneous performance of your self-appointed "inside job." Your undercover job may be as general as improving the human interactions at the workplace or as specific as influencing company safety measures.

— "Optimal Work" is simply that: finding the job that's tailor-made for you—the job you were born for. It also explores the question: Just how far can satisfaction go?

## SOFT IS HARD

The book is designed to bring the human-oriented values popularized by such writers as Gerald Jampolsky and Leo Buscaglia to bear on the workplace.

It can also be seen as presenting the job-holder's side of an emerging dialogue about the nature of work in our society. The finest current literature on management is laying an increasing stress on human values such as integrity and love. Thomas J. Peters, in his book, *The Passion for Excellence,* describes the "loose-tight" style of leadership in the top-notch companies he studied like this: "Leaders in those companies had simple, crisp and clear visions, but the intensity and clarity of the shared values behind those visions allowed lots of room for autonomy, creative expression, and love, care, and empathy." Peters sums up the attitude of the finest of modern management thus: "Soft (trust, care for people) is hard (dollars, a well-run city)."

If top management sees autonomy, creative expression, and love as important and financially rewardable qualities in the workplace, there is no lack of people who wish to see more autonomy, creativity, and caring expressed in their work. Sociologist and pollster Daniel Yankelovich, in his book, *New Rules: Searching for Self-Fulfillment in a World Turned Upside Down,* reports that an increasingly large number of people "want to participate in decisions that affect their work . . . prefer variety to routine and informality to formalism . . . want their work to be interesting as well as to pay well and to give them an outlet for creativity . . . seek responsibility and like to set their own goals . . . enjoy working in small groups. . . ." He notes "increasing evidence that the work style they prefer may be far more productive in tomorrow's service/information/high-technology economy than the work relationships of the past." This book reflects the values and attitudes of those people.

## DOING AND DREAMING

All of us have two major modes of thought, the imaginative and the realistic: we are both doers and dreamers. Since humans possess these two faculties and tend to be wholly satisfied only when both of them are appropriately exercised, it is important for people to use both faculties whenever they are thinking deeply about themselves and their work lives.

Many people, even those who are fairly creative and imaginative in their approach to their personal life, allow any sense of vision to lapse when they think about work and money. Lacking a lyrical or imaginative approach to work, they find themselves working at jobs that lack lyricism and imagination.

To help you integrate the imaginative and the realistic, the pragmatic and the visionary faculties in your approach to work, this book suggests techniques through which you can find work which is as acceptable to your highest vision as to your most basic needs and requirements; as practical and grounded in the mundane realities of the marketplace as it is playful and inspirational.

Diarist and writer Anaïs Nin expresses the balance between pragmatism and vision in these lovely and brutally realistic words: "I mastered the mechanisms of life the better to bend it to the will of the dream . . . With hammer and nails, paint, soap, money, typewriter, cookbook, douche bags, I created a dream."

# GIVING YOURSELF A "JOB PHYSICAL"

**Relevance:** Take an in-depth look at your present work situation.

**Premise:** The more you know about your passions, your values, and your skills, the easier it will be for you to find interesting and satisfying work.

**Strategy:** Give yourself a job physical. Take a look at the work you do, the work you'd like to be doing, and how you feel about the difference between them.

**Tactics:** Examine your values, interests, and delights. Identify your skill areas and work preferences. Utilize a broad range of techniques to uncover your hidden potential.

# Chapter 2

## GIVING YOURSELF A "JOB PHYSICAL"

*Without work, all life goes rotten, but when work is soulless, life stifles and dies.*

*Albert Camus*

Most people work an eight-hour day, plus travel time, five days a week. You put in all these hours for yourself and your family, of course: it's what you do to make a living. But you're usually working for someone else, in the sense that they hire you, they decide on the project, you work in their office or at their factory, and it's their product or service that gets produced. You do it for the boss, for the stockholders, for the people who pay your wages.

This chapter asks you to do some work for yourself, and put in some serious thinking about the important issues of your life, your work, and your life's work.

Most people, when they introduce themselves, say something like "Hi, I'm Bill. I'm 24 years old, single, and I'm an electronics engineer," or "I'm Linda. In five months my youngest will graduate from college. The tuition bills are about over, and I'm ready to leave the accounts receivable department at Memorial Hospital far behind." People generally describe themselves in terms of what they do for a living, but seldom mention the things that make them "come alive." Of course, that's appropriate for a first meeting; but when you give yourself a job physical, you're going to need to be conscious of yourself and what makes you come alive in a whole new way. It's not enough to know your job description. You'll need to think about your dreams and interests as well as your skills and aptitudes. Few people spend much time thinking about these issues, but those who do often gain unexpected insights.

The job physical that follows is designed to help you do just that. Like the physical you get from your doctor, your job physical is a checkup. It is a way to evaluate what's going on in your life as far as work is concerned. It doesn't imply that anything is necessarily wrong or that you'll have to make any changes: it simply lets you know what's happening.

Your decisions about work are among the most important ones you'll ever make. In fact, it's probably not an exaggeration to say that choosing the work you do is almost as important as choosing your spouse. A little focused concentration now can bring enormous dividends for the rest of your life.

How did you choose the work you have or are planning to take up? Many people find themselves working in a particular industry because someone in their family worked in the same area, or knew someone else who did. Others were told about a job by a friend. They had the contacts and were able to get a head start. Of course, these methods have their advantages. But what about the drawbacks?

In many ways, these approaches to work are like going into an arranged marriage: things may work out splendidly, and then again they may not. But there's one significant difference. People who would react vehemently against the idea of an arranged marriage often don't hesitate when it comes to an arranged job.

Other people pick their work because it's convenient—perhaps it's near their home. But even though home may be where the heart is, it doesn't necessarily follow that the work that's nearest your home is also nearest your heart.

The purpose of the job physical is to make sure that you examine all your options, whether you're in an arranged job or not, whether you have a job that needs only a little fine tuning to make it perfect, or whether you're out looking for work and want to make sure the work you wind up with is worthwhile.

## PRACTICING PSYCHOLOGICAL ENTREPRENEURSHIP

This weekend (thank God, it's Saturday) and next, we'd like you to go through this chapter very carefully, focusing on three things: yourself, your values, and work. You are going to practice a kind of psychological entrepreneurship, where you take yourself and the quality of your work into your own hands, and move forward.

You may find the exercises start to spark a lot of thought, and that it really takes you some time to work through them. You'll probably benefit from spending two Saturday afternoons on the task, because you'll be able to reflect on the issues during the week. People have their energetic days and their tired times, and going through your job physical on two separate occasions may help to even things out.

But you're not punching in on somebody else's time clock. If you finish in one afternoon, great. If it takes a couple of weekends, or even a month, that's okay. You will have the benefit of some additional time for insight and reflection.

## FOUR SELF-EXPLORATION TOOLS

From time to time, as you're going through your job physical, you may hit an area that you'd like to focus on in depth. This section offers you some tools to do that.

Each of the four techniques discussed here can help you to access your intuition, the part of you that "knows more than you realized you knew." Strongly visual people may find that "visual-ization" works best for them. Talkers and writers may prefer "journal writing" and "dialoguing." "Clustering" may work well for systems-oriented people. And "focusing" may be best for people who are used to "flying by the gut." But any method of tapping into your intuition will help, and it's worth experiment-ing to see which techniques work best for you.

These techniques may uncover feelings or attitudes you didn't know you had. Allow yourself to acknowledge contradic-tory or irrational feelings. The French philosopher Pascal said, "the heart has reasons that reason knows not of." Finding con-tradictory attitudes and feelings is a positive sign. It means you're getting close to the heart of the matter.

It's important to acknowledge and express both your positive and negative work feelings. You'll be amazed at the relief, when one of the painful feelings you haven't quite admitted comes into the open. And it can be equally helpful in bad circumstances to recall the good things, and to discover solutions to some of the problems.

Whatever techniques you choose, you need to find your own style. Discover what works best for you, and emphasize those areas you want to know more about. Enjoy the process.

• Keeping a Journal:

You may find it's useful to keep a diary while you're working through this chapter, particularly if you're uncomfortable with question-and-answer formats. The simplest way to do this is to keep your diary informal—miscellaneous jottings that you keep in a binder will do fine.

A more formal and powerful method of diary-keeping is Ira Progoff's Intensive Journal method. Progoff, a distinguished therapist and author, has devised a very structured approach to writing a diary, which he describes in his book, *At a Journal Workshop*. It includes specific methods for keeping track of your life on different time scales ranging from a daily log to the most significant moments of a whole lifetime. Tristine Rainer's book, *The New Diary,* more accessible than Progoff's book, offers a simple introduction to the art and science of journal-keeping.

Dialoguing:

One technique for self-exploration that both authors recommend is writing out a dialogue between yourself and some person, idea, or event that is important in your life. You might find it helpful, as Bill did, to start an ongoing dialogue with your work.

Bill:   Work, how are you feeling?

Work:   How do you think I'm feeling? This project was supposed to have been out the door five weeks ago, and the boss is breathing down all our necks.

Bill:   That's the short-term, and I know it's tough. But how do you feel about the long haul?

Work:   If we can just get through this project, the overtime will cut back, and things will smoothe out.

Bill:   You don't sound too convincing.

Work:   I guess I'm not all that convinced. I try to be cheerful, but I'm really feeling pretty pressured and frustrated.

Bill:   How come you try so hard to be cheerful, then?

Work:   You seem to want me to. You always want to put a happy face on things.

Bill:   Well, now I'd rather you come clean, and tell me what's really wrong.

You get the idea. Dialoguing with your work can lead you to dialogue with other parts of yourself. After a while, Bill decided to talk to that "happy face" part of himself and find out more about it.

Bill:   So what's so important about seeing the bright side?

Happy:   You have to. It's the only thing that keeps you on keel. Otherwise it's like you've failed.

Bill:   And have you?

Happy:   Yes and no. I've made mistakes, for sure, but when you're up against the kind of deadlines we're facing, you don't have much time to fix things . . .

Bill:   What if you admitted that mistakes are all part of the process?

Happy:   They'd still take up a lot of time, but I guess I wouldn't blame myself as much.

Bill:   And then would you feel better?

Happy:   Maybe I would . . .

Which sort of dialogue would suit you? A dialogue with your work? Your frustrations? Your future? Your boss (you can tackle problems with him on paper that you wouldn't want to tackle in person)? A respected and wise friend? Your own inner wisdom? Dialoguing can put you in touch with new ways to handle old problems, and reveal feelings you barely knew you had.

● Visualization:

Visualization is another technique that you might want to explore. Adelaide Bry, in her book, *Visualization,* describes it as "directing the movies of your mind." There is a great deal of evidence which suggests that deliberately "imaging" or visualizing your goals can strengthen your chances of achieving them. If this idea intrigues you, you may want to turn some of the exercises into visualizations.

What would your ideal job look like? Close your eyes, relax, and run the movie of your choice in the theater of your mind. What are you doing? Where are you doing it? See your ideal job in as much detail as you can. Imagine the desk, the bench, the tools, the view out the window. Imagine the sounds around you, the smells. Visualize the faces of the people you work with in this ideal workplace. The idea is to imagine the scene so vividly and in so much detail that if there's a clock in the room, you know what time it is.

When you're through, briefly write down what you learned: "When I asked myself what my optimal job would look like, I expected to visualize myself opening a bookkeeping service," Linda wrote. "With my background in hospital accounting, it seemed like the natural idea. But in fact, I found myself walking into an office with my name on the door, followed by the letters C.P.A. I've put two kids through college, but I've never done anything for myself. When I open my doors for business, I want to be a professional—with the credentials that that requires."

One refinement of the visualization technique is particularly helpful: Run the movies in your mind as before, but this time cast a character in your movie who represents insight and wisdom.

You might choose a favorite relative, or some other figure whom you feel comfortable with and whose wisdom you can rely on. Imagine discussing your work with that person, and ask them whatever questions you would like. Be prepared for them to give you some unexpected counsel; visualization taps into parts of your unconscious that you don't usually meet.

• Clustering:

Clustering is another powerful technique for learning more about yourself and your feelings. Gabrielle Rico describes it in her book, *Writing the Natural Way,* but you can apply the same principles to find out more about your attitudes and feelings towards your work.

The idea here is to take a central issue—"MY WORK" would be fine to begin with—and write it somewhere toward the center of a blank sheet of paper. Then start jotting down some key words that refer to all the ideas that seem to relate to your work in one way or another, even the distant cousins.

It's more important to get down a wide list of associations than it is to cover one area in detail, so don't worry if your cluster covers a large territory. Bill created a cluster that looked like this:

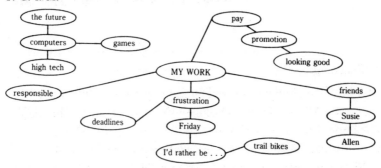

It might take a couple of minutes to write down your first cluster. It's something you should do fairly fast in order to catch some of those unexpected ideas. "Looking good" was a surprise, coming after "promotion," but it was Bill's immediate response. When "trail bikes" crossed Bill's mind, he didn't immediately write it down because he didn't think it related to work—until "Friday" and "I'd rather be . . ." convinced him.

Take a few minutes, write down your cluster, and then write a paragraph or two which deals with some of the more important issues that have come up. Bill's paragraph read:

"I love the high tech aspects of my work. I'm pleased when people ask me what I do and I can say I work in computers. I enjoy video games, remote phones, compact discs, and all the rest. In fact, I'm so keen on my job it frustrates me. I want to get ahead, and I'm good at the work I do, so I sometimes rush through things in an attempt to impress my boss. I know there's a chance of promotion coming up and I don't want to blow it. But when I hurry too much, I sometimes make stupid mistakes, and that kills me. That's when I get really frustrated. And after a while I can't focus any longer. I start daydreaming about motorcross. . . ."

You don't have to write about all the areas you touched on in your cluster, but pay special attention to the unexpected associations you came up with. They'll usually give you a clue about the places where you have ambivalent attitudes about your work. Those are the areas to look at to gain further insight into what might lead to greater job satisfaction.

- Focusing:

Another technique you might want to try was introduced by University of Chicago psychologist Eugene Gendlin in his book, *Focusing.* Focusing is a simple, six-part process, designed to get you in touch with your feelings rather than your ideas.

First, give yourself what Gendlin calls "space." Relax, close your eyes, and let your immediate thoughts, worries, and concerns drift away. Let yourself slow down, and pay attention to the part of your body that you "feel" with, perhaps your stomach or chest. Then ask yourself a question that relates to a problem area, such as, "How do I feel about my new boss?" Let the answer well up from a sensing in your own body. When you get an answer, don't jump into the feeling. Simply recognize that there's an issue there, and ask yourself what else you feel. Repeat this process four or five times, until you've tapped into the main issues surrounding that problem area.

Second, discover what Gendlin calls your "felt sense." Select one of the issues that came up for you, and pay attention again to the "feeling place" inside you as you sense what the issue feels like. Don't step into the feeling, just let it be there.

Third, give your felt sense a "handle." Ask yourself what this feeling is like, and notice the words that come into your mind. "Tight," "cornered," "stuck at a desk at age seven" are some phrases that might come up. Keep asking yourself for phrases until you find one that feels just right.

Fourth, let the handle you've chosen "resonate" with your feeling. Go back and forth between the felt sense and the words. Your sense or feeling may change, or you may find a different word or phrase. When your word feels just right for your body's sense of the problem area, they're resonating together.

Fifth, sense your feeling again, and "ask" yourself what it is about your problem that makes the handle you've come up with so right. "Why does my new boss remind me so much of sitting at a desk at age seven?" Stay in contact with your overall sense of the problem. If you find yourself giving an answer that doesn't make that felt sense shift in some way, go back to your sense, and ask again. "Ah, there it is. He sometimes reacts to people who don't agree with him by belittling them . . . tries to make you feel like a dumb kid. . . ." When you get an answer from the feeling itself, you'll be able to sense that there's been a small release.

Sixth, when an answer comes up, no matter how unexpected, that causes a "shift" in your sense of the problem, welcome it and stay with it for a minute or two. Then go back to the start of the process, and begin to track down some other aspect of the problem.

You won't reach a shift every time you focus, and that's fine. But when you do, you will have learned something about your feelings and released some energy that was previously locked up in the problem.

These four techniques will help you to explore areas that you want to pay special attention to. You probably won't want to use all four methods all of the time, but they may help you to work through some of the questions in your job physical, particularly in areas where you feel stuck.

Now let's look at the ground rules for the job physical itself.

## HOW TO TAKE THE JOB PHYSICAL

As you go through the rest of this chapter, it's important to follow the instructions, answer the questions as honestly as you can, and above all, not give up. Some of the questions concern the way you feel about your work. Some investigate the kind of person you are. Some deal with the concrete details of your actual work situation.

Here are some different ways to approach this task. What's important is to find the style that suits you best.

— Some people do this kind of thing best when they're entirely alone with the telephone off the hook, and a "do not disturb" sign posted.

— Others know that if they have to answer a whole lot of questions out of a book, they'll get bored and distracted. They do much better if they have a friend to ask them the questions, and draw them out when they feel stuck.

— Another approach you can take with a friend is to have them answer some of the questions as if they were speaking for you, and to compare their answers with your own. There may be ways in which your friends see you more accurately than you see yourself.

— Some people find they can get the most from this process by writing out their answers. There are lots of things we already know in a quiet way, and writing them down often brings them front and center.

— Still others find it's handy to use a tape recorder and speak off the cuff, and then listen afterward to what they said. It may be a case of, "How can I know what I think till I hear what I say?"

Those are the possibilities. We strongly recommend that you adopt one of the last two options. Just sitting back and thinking your way through the chapter won't give you the creative opportunity that writing down your answers or speaking them out loud will. Also, whether you write, speak, or type, it is important to keep a record of your process, and file your notes away in a safe place. You'll want them later. If you're writing, don't worry about how well it reads. You're doing this to discover more about yourself and your work, not to create a literary masterpiece.

If you are just entering the job market, or are currently unemployed, some of the questions won't seem to apply to you.

When the questions are about "present work," rephrase them, and answer them either in terms of the kind of work you'd like to do, or of your last or most important job. The questions about "ideal work" should apply to you as they stand.

• Public and Private Faces:

When things aren't going too well, people often like to put on a brave face. And, conversely, when we are really delighted, we often behave nonchalantly, and are reluctant to show too much enthusiasm. It's a perfectly normal tendency—but you need to be honest about your situation if you are to be able to improve it.

As you go through the rest of this chapter, don't gloss over things that make you feel deeply uncomfortable, and don't act cool about things that really excite you. You may have contradictory feelings about your work. You may feel confused about some things, enraged about others. As far as you can manage it, don't censor yourself: let *all* your insights and feelings emerge.

You don't have to answer every question. This is not a rigorous test, and no one is going to grade you for completeness. But do read through the entire chapter to find the questions that are most relevant to you. The purpose is to stir your thought processes, not to persuade you to take any immediate action. If one or two questions trigger new insights for you, they may be of more benefit than a painstaking approach to the whole questionnaire. Remember, there are no right or wrong answers.

## PART ONE: A QUICK OVERVIEW OF YOUR VALUES

The first section of the job physical offers you a chance to get a basic sense of the values that are most important in your life. Your values are an important part of you; they don't change just because your job does. Work satisfaction happens when your values and dreams coincide with your work. It's that simple.

Dr. Jeylan T. Mortimer, professor of sociology at the University of Minnesota, recently made a study of work attitudes and found that the most important single factor influencing job satisfaction was "work autonomy": the employee's sense that he or she can make their own decisions and influence what happens in the workplace.

Although other studies have said the same thing, what made Dr. Mortimer's study unusual was her finding that income had no significant effect on job satisfaction. Though people in high-income jobs generally have more autonomy than those who earn less, Dr. Mortimer found that people with equivalent levels of autonomy appeared to be equally happy with their jobs, regardless of differences of income. Valuing "autonomy" more highly than "financial security" would seem to be an attitude that leads to greater job satisfaction.

In another study, Suzanne Kobasa, a psychologist at the City University of New York, tracked 200 AT&T executives for ten years to find out which values affected their ability to handle stress, and their general health. She found that those executives who expressed a strong sense of three key values coped better with stress, and were half as likely to get sick as their colleagues. The values were:

**Commitment**    to the job, one's spouse or family, or to social institutions and personal integrity.

**Challenge**    seeing change, difficulties, and problems as challenges to be met and overcome.

**Control**    over one's life and work.

Let's take a specific look, now, at your own values as they relate to work issues. As you answer these questions, you will begin to recognize your work values and provide a context in which to examine your working life in detail.

— What is it that gives your work life the greatest sense of meaning and purpose? Commitment? Challenge? Control? What else?

— Creativity, perhaps?

— Knowing that you've performed well under pressure?

— Working well with others?

— Beating out the competition?

— The faith that your work makes a contribution to society?

— What are you striving for, above all else, in your working life? How do your ambitions express your sense of values?

## PART TWO: WORK INVENTORY

This section draws your attention to issues which relate to the work you are currently doing, or to the last job you had.

We intend to focus mainly on the positive, but we shall also address problems and dissatisfactions. Getting a realistic grasp of where the problems lie is a necessary first step toward resolving them.

Feel free, whether you are answering these questions with a friend or by yourself, to expand on any issues that seem particularly relevant, and to answer those extra questions in each section which bear on your specific circumstances. Make sure, at the end of each section, to sum up what you've learned in a sentence or two.

Later in the book, we shall come back to many of these issues in more detail. For the moment though, the idea is simply to raise the issues, and to note areas that could use some improvement.

Don't make any major decisions, or suddenly decide to switch jobs while you're reading this chapter. You're exploring your feelings and attitudes, not deciding on a course of action. If you begin to feel you want to look for other work, don't be hasty. Major changes can come later, when you've read the rest of this book, thought about the issues in some detail, and talked them over with your spouse, family, or friends.

- Facts at the Ground Level:

Let's look at the way you feel about your job.

— How did you get into this job?

— What aspects of the job attracted you to it in the first place?

— Overall, do you privately love, enjoy, tolerate, dislike, or hate your work?

— Which aspects of your work do you particularly enjoy?

— Which aspects do you particularly dislike?

— When your friends talk about their work, what kinds of jobs sound interesting?

— Does any part of your job give you an opportunity to do that kind of work?

— What did you want to be when you were a kid—and more importantly, what aspects of those dreams if any still appeal to you?

Your answers to these questions can show you a great deal about your present level of job satisfaction. Notice any correlations you may find between the answers. For example, ask yourself whether the aspects of the job that attracted you in the first place are still the ones you most enjoy, or whether they have become the ones you now most dislike.

Use your answers to these questions to get a sense of what's right, and wrong, with your present work. Then sum up what you've learned in a sentence or two. For example, "I got into real estate because I needed the flexible hours, and that's still a plus for me. But on the weekends, when I'd like to be doing something with my family, I sometimes resent how long the hours can be." By summarizing at the end of each section of the job physical, you are taking the pulse of your work, and getting an overall picture of the many issues involved.

• Exploring the Work Itself:

Now let's look at the various aspects of your job and your workplace, to define how you really feel about your work life.

The degree of challenge and stimulation you feel on the job is a major factor in work satisfaction. People who feel their work lacks sufficient challenge tend to "cut out" from boredom, while those who feel the challenges are too great also "cut out," this time from overload. Think about your work, and ask yourself the following questions:

— Is it unpredictable? Stimulating? Difficult to get on top of?

— Is it challenging? Interpersonally? Creatively? Intellectually?

— Is there enough responsibility? Too little? Too much?

— Do you hope to move up in your organization, and if so, are there opportunities for you to do so?

— Do new technological advances in your field fascinate you? Intimidate you?

— How often do you learn something new on the job?

— Overall, how do these issues influence your feelings about your work situation?

Write down a sentence or two that summarizes what you've learned from these questions. "I enjoy the technical challenges in my work, but sometimes feel I don't have enough personal responsibility."

● Your Pay:

Somewhat paradoxically, being paid isn't really a part of work. Pay is something you receive as a result of the work you do. The questions in this section have to do with how you feel about the exchange you make for your work and time.

— Do you feel you are paid what you are worth?

— Do you feel you are paid appropriately for the job you do?

— How much more do you think you should earn for the job you do? Are you likely to get that much from your present employer?

— How flexible are you about your income?

— How close is your pay to what you would describe as satisfactory?

Write a paragraph summarizing what you've learned from these questions.

● The People You Work With:

Your coworkers can make a greater difference to your job satisfaction than the work itself. Friends in the workplace can make a dull job tolerable, and a tolerable job very pleasant. And one person that you have a really hard time getting along with can be enough to make you want to give up the job.

— Are the people you work with easy to get along with?

— Are they people you respect professionally?

— Do you enjoy their company at work?

— Are they friends, or potential friends?

— If some of them are hard to get along with, does that make doing your work difficult?

— How much of the problem is outside your control?

— How are your relationships with those "above" you?

— How do you get on with the people you supervise?

Your coworkers can be the "make or break" element in your day. If these are issues you want to work on in more detail, try a dialogue with a coworker or boss.

• Your Workplace:

Few people know much about the place they'll be working in until they turn up for the first day on the job. Yet the environment you work in can have a major impact on how much you enjoy your work.

— Is your workplace comfortable and aesthetically pleasing?

— Is the equipment up-to-date, safe, and efficient?

— Is your workplace a healthy environment in terms of lighting, ventilation, noise?

— Do you enjoy being in your place of business?

If this is an issue you'd like to explore in greater detail, try visualizing your "ideal workplace."

• Your Product or Service:

If you wouldn't recommend the product you deal in to your best friend, the chances are you don't feel too good about your work. In a very real sense, it's the product you make (or the service you offer) that gives real meaning to your work.

— How do you feel about the product or service you are involved in producing, advertising, selling, distributing?

— Do you feel it makes a positive contribution to society? If not, does this concern you?

— Are there ways in which this product or service could be improved that would make you feel better about it?

— Can you influence or contribute in some way to these changes?

Summarize your feelings on these issues in a brief paragraph. Use focusing or clustering to explore this area in more detail.

• Your Company:

Right behind the product stands the company. Once again, it's hard to feel satisfied in your work if you feel at odds with the company for whom you work.

— Are you in agreement with your company's aims and objectives?

— Do you feel positive about the company's treatment of its employees, its clients, and its consumers?

— Do you feel comfortable with your company's business practices?

Try focusing to find out a bit more about the way you feel. After all, they say that you can tell someone's character by the company they keep.

You have now covered the basics of your work situation: what you do, who you do it with, where, and how you feel about it. Each of these issues has a bearing on work satisfaction, but some of them will seem more important than others. As you come to the end of the section, decide which questions highlighted both the most positive and most negative aspects of your work. These are the issues where you have the most to gain and the most to lose, and around which the most beneficial changes can occur.

## PART THREE: SELF-INVENTORY

In this section, the emphasis is on you and what you bring to your work, rather than on the work itself.

Few things are as difficult as forming an objective picture of oneself. Most people tend to have a fairly firm picture of their character and nature. But as the merest slip of the tongue, psychoanalysis, and hypnosis attest, unconscious feelings can emerge. The factors you hide from yourself are very often the ones that block and frustrate your efforts to find more reward in your work.

This entire section of self-inventory is one which you may want to discuss with a friend or spouse. You may even find it helpful to ask them to go through all the questions with you, and answer them on your behalf, using their own sense of your talents and attitudes.

• Your Skills and Talents:

The first part of this inventory is designed to reveal your skills and abilities by reminding you of the aspects of your life which may have given rise to them.

— What skills or qualifications did you bring to the job?

— What abilities or expertise have you developed on the job?

— What talents have you developed as a result of hobbies, working in or around the house, playing and interacting with your children, or doing community work?

— What attributes do your friends notice and compliment you on?

These questions may remind you of some skills you would normally overlook. To help you get a more detailed picture of your talents and skill areas, we suggest that you rate yourself in each category listed below on the 0–5 scale provided; 0 meaning you have virtually no skills, and 5 meaning you are highly skilled.

Ability to motivate people:     0..1..2..3..4..5

Artistic talents:     0..1..2..3..4..5

Budgeting:     0..1..2..3..4..5

Capacity to make decisions:     0..1..2..3..4..5

Caring skills:     0..1..2..3..4..5

Clerical:     0..1..2..3..4..5

Consulting to groups:     0..1..2..3..4..5

Counseling individuals:     0..1..2..3..4..5

Dealing with data:     0..1..2..3..4..5

Delegation of authority:     0..1..2..3..4..5

Design skills:     0..1..2..3..4..5

Detail work:     0..1..2..3..4..5

Evaluating skills:     0..1..2..3..4..5

Functioning under stress:    0..1..2..3..4..5

Imagination:    0..1..2..3..4..5

Initiative and leadership:    0..1..2..3..4..5

Innovation:    0..1..2..3..4..5

Knowledge of resources:    0..1..2..3..4..5

Listening skills:    0..1..2..3..4..5

Manual dexterity:    0..1..2..3..4..5

Negotiation:    0..1..2..3..4..5

Networking:    0..1..2..3..4..5

Operating machines:    0..1..2..3..4..5

Outdoor work:    0..1..2..3..4..5

Planning skills:    0..1..2..3..4..5

Public speaking ability:    0..1..2..3..4..5

Record keeping:    0..1..2..3..4..5

Sales:    0..1..2..3..4..5

Simplifying what is complex:    0..1..2..3..4..5

Survival skills:    0..1..2..3..4..5

Teaching and coaching skills:    0..1..2..3..4..5

Time management:    0..1..2..3..4..5

Writing skills:    0..1..2..3..4..5

It's possible to break skill areas down into more and more detailed levels. It will help you to get a clearer picture of your abilities if you note any additional skills that the listed areas suggested to you.

Now let's take this a step further. Quickly go back through the list and rate which skills you really enjoy using. Are they the same as the ones you're most skilled at? What areas combine the maximum of skill and enjoyment? Which skills are you most interested in developing?

Your most developed skills are the ones that are likely to be most marketable, and the skills you enjoy using are the ones that will bring you most satisfaction. For complete job satisfaction, you need a good mix of both.

● Your Interests:

Your interests and passions can often tell you more about yourself than either your actual work or a listing of your skills. Some people choose the work they do because of their interests, while others keep work and personal interests in separate compartments. But again, only when work overlaps with interests and passions are you likely to feel interested in it, or passionate about it.

Make a list of your areas of interest, and then ask yourself the following questions:

— Which of these areas are you able to pursue in the course of your work?

— Which ones have some tangential relevance to the work you do?

— Which do you pursue in your spare time?

— Which outside concerns are you currently not pursuing at all? Why?

— Which of your interests would you like to see incorporated into your work?

— Which ones would you specifically like to keep separate from your paid work? Why?

Summarize your findings in a paragraph, and try using a technique such as visualization or clustering to explore these areas more fully.

● Your Work Style:

The following questions will help you discover the working style that you prefer:

— Do you prefer doing work you've already mastered to working in areas where there's still a lot to learn?

— Do you like working on a long-term project, or on a series of short-term projects?

— Do you prefer to work alone or on a team?

— Do you get more accomplished when you are solely responsible for a particular project?

— Do your fellow team members help spark your creativity or productivity?

— How much competition do you like at work?

— How much supervision do you like?

— Do you enjoy managing others?

Summarize the most important points you have learned from this set of questions. "I've realized how much pleasure working on a team gives me. I can get a lot accomplished by myself, but having other people to bounce my ideas off really ups the quality."

● Your Time:

Your sense of time can have a great deal to do with how you feel about your work.

— Do you have enough time to do the work you are expected to accomplish?

— Does your work leave you enough time to enjoy the other parts of your life?

— Are you always running into crises at work?

— Are these crises of your own making, or dictated by circumstances outside your control?

— Do you accomplish more or less when you set your own schedule? Why?

— Are you glad to work overtime?

— Would you rather take work home with you or stay late at the office to finish?

Did any of these questions touch on a raw spot? That may indicate something you need to think about changing either in your attitude, or in your work.

• Your Health and Well-being:

Listening to your body may tell you something you won't hear anywhere else. These questions not only target actual work-related health problems, they also offer you another means of evaluating the way you feel about your work in general.

— How frequently do you feel exhilarated after a day's work?

— How often do you feel deeply satisfied or at peace?

— What aspects of your day contribute to these feelings?

— Do you often feel physically and/or emotionally drained when you come home from work?

— Do you feel particularly bad before, during, or after specific kinds of work?

— Is stress a frequent problem?

— Has your body been sending you signals?

Your health is an important factor in your work. If you feel your work has been adversely affecting your health, you may want to zero in on the issue with one of the techniques described at the beginning of the chapter.

Now pick out the two or three most important issues in your self-inventory. Give special attention to any areas where you really came alive, or slumped down in your chair, while you were working on this section. You will need to pay particular attention to these issues as you consider the strategies and techniques offered in the rest of the book.

## PART FOUR: IN-DEPTH PROBE

By the time you've completed the previous parts of this questionnaire, you will have considered most of the major issues that come up in connection with your work. The last section is designed to uncover some of the hidden dynamics that influence your experience of work.

There are two steps to any kind of change: knowing what's wrong, and doing something about it. You want to get a very clear fix on the things that need changing before you start deciding what to do about them. You also want to be clear about those facets which are either fine the way they are, or could be expanded or enhanced.

This section raises very few new issues, but it differs from the earlier sections in terms of how you will be dealing with them.

• Sentence Completion:

One method of probing into your attitudes is the technique of repeated sentence completion, pioneered by Dr. Nathaniel

Branden in his book, *If You Could Hear What I Cannot Say*. Dr. Branden is a psychotherapist who has discovered that people store their truths in layers, much like the layers of an onion. His technique is designed to help you peel away at the surface layers to get at some of your deeper truths.

The idea is to take each of the following incomplete sentences and fill in the blank. Then go back to the original lead phrase, fill in the blank again, go back, complete the sentence again, and again. You will probably want to chose just a couple of sentence fragments from each section, and then answer each one a number of times. But if you come across a question that really stirs something up inside, you may want to keep on plugging until you feel you've exhausted all your responses. For example, you might talk about your new job like this:

— One reason I enjoy my work is that . . .
   . . . it pays the mortgage

— One reason I enjoy my work is that . . .
   . . . it lets me shine
   . . . I meet clients I like
   . . . the people I work with are interesting

— One reason I enjoy my work is that . . .
   . . . I can use my talents and enthusiasm
   . . . it puts all my education to good use
   . . . I'm learning new skills every day
   . . . it gives me predictability
   . . . I don't know

— One reason I enjoy my work is that . . .
   . . . all in all, it makes me feel I contribute.

If you decide to do this exercise in writing, you should write as quickly as possible and go back to the lead phrase immediately, without any pause, and start over. The idea is to allow yourself complete spontaneity. It doesn't matter whether all your answers are accurate, or whether they contradict one another. Don't stop to worry about it if your mind gets stuck. Invent an answer. Keep on going until you have at least ten completions for every lead phrase.

Try to keep your sentence completions short, as they were in the example; no wandering off into long explanations. And feel free to exaggerate: some of the deepest truths come forth when we deliberately overstate the case.

This technique works extremely well when you have a close friend with you to lead you through the questions. Your friend should sit facing you, look into your eyes, and listen carefully. It is not your partner's job to respond, doubt you, disagree, or judge you in any way. He or she is there to provide you with that rare luxury: a willing, sensitive audience.

When you or your partner notice that you are feeling some kind of strong emotion, you should pause for a minute or two, and just sit, letting the feeling be present. If you brush aside your feelings too rapidly, you may miss some truth you might have learned from them.

It's also important for you to allow yourself to draw positive conclusions from any negative feelings that may arise. When you have the sense that some kind of a breakthrough is taking place, you should switch to a lead phrase that allows you to come to a positive conclusion, such as

— I'm beginning to see that . . .

— I never quite told myself before that . . .

— I'm reluctantly beginning to admit that . . .

Let's take an example.
Suppose you're doing a sentence completion exercise and a

strong negative emotion comes up. Let's say you are complet-ing the sentence, "One part of my work that I really can't stand is . . . ," and you say, "when the manager faults me for being slow." When you feel a surge of negative emotion, go back and complete the sentence again, this time expressing yourself in more detail: "One part of my work that I really can't stand is when I take the time to make sure cranky cus-tomers are really cared for, and then the manager faults me for being too slow. I blow a fuse somewhere and feel totally trapped. . . ." That "trapped" feeling may well up inside you as you say the word. Let the feeling be there for a minute or two. Allow yourself to feel it.

Then turn to one of the lead sentences that allows you to translate that negative emotion into a positive intention. "I need to make sure I don't get carried away talking with customers," or, "I'm beginning to see that I need to trust myself more," or, "I shouldn't be so hard on myself." When you've paused for a while, and drawn some kind of conclusion, go back to the exercise.

● The Why Technique:

Whenever you want a change of pace, or feel you are getting close to an area that needs exploring, you can probe your sen-tence completion further by using the "why" technique.

The idea here is to read the lead statements and fill in the blank, and then probe your choice by asking yourself, "why?" Ask yourself "why?" again and again, until the answers begin to reveal things you didn't know about yourself.

As you will see from the following example, you need to be flexible about this. Sometimes a different question will reveal more than you'd learn by just repeating "why?" Again, don't work too hard at making the whole thing logical and consistent, this is an exercise in digging for the unexpected. Above all, be spontaneous.

Bill, as you may have noticed when he did his clustering

exercise, has a problem with deadlines. Here's an example of the way he might use the "why" technique to investigate the issue.

— When I'm up against a deadline, I . . .
   tend to do my best work.

— Why?
   Because I know the crunch is on.

— Why is the crunch on?
   I guess because I let it happen.

— Do you enjoy it? [new question]
   I suppose in a way I do, but I hate it, too.

— Then why do you let it get that far?
   Maybe I'm lazy.

— Why are you lazy?
   No, I don't think it's laziness, really. I guess after each crunch I need time to relax.

— Why's that?
   I'm always dead tired after a crisis.

— Why?
   I bring it on myself, I suppose. It has to do with thinking I work best in a crisis.

— Well then? [new question]
   I see I have pretty contradictory feelings about deadlines. I tend to bring them down on my own head, and then complain about them.

— Why?
   If I like deadlines so much, why don't I enjoy them? Maybe I don't really enjoy them. Perhaps I would be happier if I didn't let things get to a crisis point.

- General Feelings About Work:

Let's begin with some overview questions about the way you feel about work in general. Here are the lead phrases:

— One thing I like about my work is . . .

— I'm most creative in my work when I . . .

— One thing I don't like so much about my work is . . .

— I feel terrible about work when I . . .

— The most interesting part of my work is . . .

— The least challenging part of my job is . . .

— I feel my work makes a real contribution when . . .

- Your Personal Opinion Poll:

Sometimes the opinions that other people hold about your work can have a very marked impact on you. Everybody is surprised from time to time to find that someone else appreciates a quality in them that they don't see in themselves. Those unexpected compliments are clues to the way some people undervalue themselves.

On the other hand, when others actively undervalue you, it's harder for you to value yourself. Either way, there's a direct impact on your chances of work satisfaction. Explore how this issue affects your work with some more sentence completions.

— I think my spouse's feeling about my work is . . .

— When my parents (friends) tell me how they view my job, I feel . . .

— Society's attitudes about the kind of work I do give me the feeling that . . .

● Time:

Time may be a major factor in your feelings about work. You examined some of your attitudes toward time in the self-inventory. Now let's take it a step further and examine your feelings, not about clocks and time cards, but about the way you perceive time.

See if you can discover what makes the difference between the hurried moments and the hours when everything seems to be flowing, between the days that pass in a flash, and the slow, fatiguing ones.

Here are some lead sentences.

— When things are slow at work, I . . .

— When I'm up against a deadline, I . . .

— Time really drags when I'm . . .

— I lose track of time when I'm . . .

— Generally, my feeling about time on the job is . . .

● Money:

Money is another area that you've already looked at. Since it's an area around which many people have very strong feelings, it may be worth using the sentence completion technique to explore it more deeply.

— Sometimes, when I think about money, I feel . . .

— When I talk to others about money, I . . .

— When I need to talk to the boss about money, I . . .

— If I didn't have to worry about money, I'd . . .

● Wrapping It Up:

These last few sentence completions will give you a chance to summarize everything you've learned so far from this chapter. Your purpose is to bring together the different strands that have arisen in the course of this questionnaire—your values, your job, your skills and enthusiasms—and to pick out the central patterns.

— I often thank God it's Friday because . . .

— I'd look forward to Monday if . . .

— My fantasy of the perfect assignment would be . . .

— Success to me means . . .

— The work I do is most worthwhile when . . .

— I guess I make things difficult for myself at work when I . . .

— Something important that hasn't come up in this exercise, is . . .

— The way I really feel about my work is . . .

Remember to close with some sentence completions that state your new discoveries and draw positive conclusions.

— I'm beginning to see that I . . .

— What I'm discovering about my work is that . . .

— I would be more effective at my job if I . . .

— It's good to know that the way I do my work is . . .

— It's wonderful to realize that the work I do means . . .

## POSITIVE WORRYING

That's your job physical: a voyage in search of a deeper understanding of yourself and your attitude toward work. Turn your discoveries and surprises over in your mind. Be glad about the positive things you've realized about yourself and others. And if you came across some problem areas that feel unresolved, don't let them gnaw at you. Instead, try "positive worrying."

Deliberately worry at them from time to time, the way a dog worries at a bone. The dog isn't worried, it's the bone that's in trouble. Think about your problems creatively, as problems that can be solved. Meditate on them, sleep on them, digest them, let them teach you.

And accept yourself, contradictions and all. You have a right to mixed feelings. The more you accept yourself, the more able you will be to change what needs to be changed.

# MONEY AND SATISFACTION

**Relevance:** You need to examine your attitudes toward money, attitudes which often seem like such self-evident truths that you seldom stop to rethink them.

**Premise:** Money is the first and most tangible level of satisfaction that a job can bring you.

**Strategy:** Make sure you are comfortable with the balance you strike between the money you make and the things you do to make it.

**Tactics:** Uncover underlying attitudes toward money, both having it, and not.

# Chapter 3

# MONEY AND SATISFACTION

*I'm opposed to millionaires, but it would be dangerous to offer me the position.*

*Mark Twain*

"Trust in God, but first tie your camel" is the advice of the prophet Mohammed. This sage piece of advice recommends both idealism and practicality, yet human beings seldom seem to manage both at once. The pragmatists among us often accuse idealists of being naive, while idealists rebuke the pragmatists for lacking moral values. Practicality and idealism are both important aspects of the full human being, and both sides of our nature need to be satisfied if the whole human is to be satisfied.

This chapter deals with practical issues; and in the job market, a big part of that practicality comes down to one word: money. There are three issues here. The first has to do with getting paid and covering your expenses; the second concerns your attitudes to money, and the ways in which they influence your choices; and the third deals with the trade-offs you are prepared to make in the process of making a living.

## COVERING YOUR BASES

For work to be satisfactory at the first and most basic level, it must provide sufficient funding to cover necessities. Naturally, there are as many ideas about what constitutes a necessity as there are individuals, but under the general rubric of tying one's camel, we include such things as

(a) the basics: food, clothing, and shelter

(b) payment of debts

(c) other necessary expenses, such as education

(d) capitalization, when required

(e) some measure of future stability, and

(f) some funding for delight, entertainment, and growth.

This last component is an important one, and one which is often undervalued; for it is delight that generates enthusiasm, and enthusiasm which is the fuel of all other forms of success. Put simply, for work to be satisfactory your pay must cover more than the basics. Money is not everything, but it can be, as the writer Somerset Maugham observed, "the sixth sense which enables you to enjoy the other five."

Ask a friend how much money they suppose it would take for them to be definitively rich. It's a lighthearted question between friends, a game, if you like. But like most games, it offers you a model of reality that you can play with. The results can be illuminating.

Most people, when asked this question, answer with a fairly substantial estimate. Then, after a little thinking, they come up with a somewhat higher figure. And if the discussion goes on for some time, they wind up with a final figure that far exceeds their first estimate.

People who start out feeling that $100,000 would be enough

to turn the scales often end up thinking in terms of a million dollars. Those who start out at the figure of a million frequently decide that they would need a million earning interest, and the million dollar home they've dreamed of, and perhaps a million dollars more to work with to create a business. The final estimate usually has much more horse sense to it than the first.

In the same way, if you ask people how much they really need, they will usually quote a figure that is about 10–15 percent higher than their current earnings. Most people hope that their next raise will move them into comfortable economic circumstances. Somehow, it's always the next raise. The implication here is that however much you earn, you're still likely to feel a little pinched.

Let's take a look at your own financial picture: your genuine needs, your comfort and security, and your idea of real wealth. Get out a pencil and paper, and do some rough budgeting.

— How much money would it take for you simply to survive?

— How much would it take for you to feel comfortable about your financial situation?

— How much would it take for you to be rich?

Your answers in dollars aren't important. But it is worth exploring the criteria you used to arrive at your answers, and some of the implications of the answers you gave.

— What went through your mind as you were answering these questions about different levels of need and financial security?

— Did you consider specific things—travel, education, buying a house? Did you think about putting your children through college? Health insurance? Retirement?

— What assumptions did you make about what you needed in order to survive?

— What did comfort or security mean to you, over and above covering your necessities?

— What did you think about when you were figuring out what it would mean for you to be genuinely rich?

## WHAT IS MONEY? A QUESTION OF ATTITUDE

Attitudes about money cover a wide range. They go from one extreme where people behave as though getting paid is the only form of satisfaction, to the other where they may discount the importance of income almost completely. Neither extreme leads to satisfactory results in the long run. The reason is simple: "Man does not live by bread alone," but neither can he live without it. The idealist tends to wind up underfed, while the pragmatist winds up undernourished.

You have briefly considered both your real financial needs and your projections. Now let's explore your attitudes and emotional feelings on the subject of money. Your goal here is to recognize your attitudes, and notice the ways in which your emotions get in the way of real satisfaction, or propel you toward it.

While you're going through this section, bear in mind that the ultimate question is going to concern the way you balance the money you make with what you're willing to do to make it. The fewer unquestioned beliefs you have about money, the easier it will be for you to balance considerations of pay against the other satisfactions that your work can offer you.

Few things have been as difficult for humans to accomplish as getting far enough into space to get a glimpse of the spherical world on which we live. The reason is that we have to get away from the earth's gravity long enough to do it. Money is often in such short supply compared to our wishes, that it is usually easier for us to want it, or need it, or go out and work for it, than it is for us to step back and understand it. Not that money is so difficult to understand. It's just that, like gravity, it often holds us too close to get a good look at it.

We can say that money is a medium for exchange, that it is a form of energy, that it is designed to serve us. By looking at several different ways in which we often think about money, we may be able to distance ourselves from it long enough to glimpse some of its possibilities, both positive and negative.

Most attitudes toward money are formed when people are quite young. As a result, the questions here may seem oversimplified. But simple matters can prove to be enormously important. The emotions that are attached to those early opinions about money can have a continuing effect throughout your life, so read the next section as though you were considering these issues for the first time. Your goal here is to make your invisible attitudes visible. Then you can keep them or change them as you choose.

• Time Is Money:

Salesmen say this to their clients when they are explaining how a laborsaving device can eliminate unnecessary work. Bosses say it when they begin to notice that some of their employees are taking long coffee breaks. "Time is money" is a phrase we use to encourage efficiency. It can even be seen as the basic rationale behind mass production. If you can make three items in the time you used to spend making two, that's an efficient use of time.

But what else can "time is money" tell us?

When you have the time, you may not have the money to enjoy it. When you have the money, you may no longer have the time. "Time is money" means that it is your time, the time of your life, that you exchange for the money you need. It means that the money you receive needs to be worth the time you spend obtaining it. And "time is money" also means that the money you earn can buy you time. Money, literally speaking, needs to buy you back the time of your life.

- Money Is Power:

Money is a means of exchange; that's what the "buying power" of your dollar means. It gets you into the ball game or the concert. It's the nothing that gets you something. Hardly anyone has used money as wallpaper, at least since the end of the Confederacy.

But we often use money as far more than a simple medium of exchange. We use it to prove ourselves worthy, to obtain or signal our status, and to give ourselves a sense of security. Money also has the power to influence and to get things done.

- Money Is Energy:

Some people claim that money is energy. If you think in those terms, it may help to remember that energy comes in two forms: potential, or stored energy (as in the energy of a new battery in a tape recorder), and kinetic, or working energy (the energy that actually runs the tape recorder).

Those who say that money is energy often say, too, that energy is nothing unless it is used. They conclude that money is nothing until it is spent. There's a certain truth in that; there's certainly not much pleasure in the idea that your life savings may wind up as estate taxes after you're gone. But if money is really a form of energy, then money in the bank (as a form of potential energy) may be just as important as "spending money" or kinetic energy.

- Money Is Like Water:

Another popular way of expressing the idea that money needs to be used suggests that money is like water. This may simply mean that, like water, it slips through your fingers. But it can also imply that money is fine when it is allowed to flow, but stagnant when it collects in one place.

Again, this idea makes a point. The immediate spender and the investment broker both suggest that money should be put to use, that it should be kept in motion. But how and when should it be spent? When is it more useful to save some for later use?

Is your preference to live on the interest your income earns when you've saved enough of it to invest? Should you spend it as fast as it comes in and enjoy it now? Or does your answer lie in some balance of these two approaches? Finally, how close do you come to your ideal balance?

● Money Is God:

Few people openly subscribe to this idea, but many behave as if they do. Many more acknowledge that it sometimes seems as if having money is right up there with cleanliness, next to godliness.

Do you worry that economic insecurity somehow proves that you aren't a good person? If so, this might be a good place to stop and do some more sentence completions. Remember to complete each sentence as many times as you can, writing quickly, and letting the ideas pour out onto the page.

— When I notice that someone isn't very well paid, I tend to feel . . .

— When I think about the unemployed, I feel . . .

— When I think about very poor people, I feel . . .

— When I think about the very rich, I feel . . .

— When I don't make enough myself to make ends meet, I feel . . .

Remember to finish up with a sentence or two that gives you room to summarize what you have learned:

— I'm beginning to understand . . .

- Money Is the Root of All Evil:

This is one of those ideas that can influence you for years without ever quite coming to the surface. Plenty of people believe that making a lot of money is a dirty business (we talk about people being "filthy rich"), and yet they blame themselves for not making enough. This is a tidy example of "Damned if you do, and damned if you don't."

— What sorts of negative feelings do you have about yourself where the subject of money is concerned?

— Would you feel badly if you suddenly received a large sum of money?

- Money Can Buy Anything:

This is so nearly true that it's dangerous. Let's take a closer look at this by contrasting it with another idea that's somehow kitty-corner to it.

- The Best Things in Life Are Free:

Falling in love. Good health. Creativity. Friends. These are probably some of the best things life has to offer. Yet even the things that money supposedly can't buy often require money. Good health is a priceless gift—but the cost of an annual physical is no small matter.

Once again, you may be surprised to find that at different times you believe in one or the other idea. In fact, you may even believe them simultaneously.

Make a list of the things you really enjoy. How many of them require relatively large amounts of money? Which of them can be enjoyed at little or no cost?

— One priceless thing about my life is . . .

— Wonderful things in my life that are free include . . .

— When I look at these things, I begin to understand . . .

- Money Is a Good Servant, But a Lousy Boss:

This is the crux of the matter. Money is useful for what it can obtain. It is the way we survive. It is the means we use to enrich our lives, as the very word "enrich" implies. It can also be a destructive obsession. We speak of people being "eaten up" by financial worries. When money rules life, there is very little left of life that is worth living.

— One way money tends to run me around is . . .

— I tend to be confused by money when . . .

— If I could only stop worrying about money, I'd . . .

— I am beginning to see that my attitudes to money . . .

— In the future I intend to . . .

- Money Is What You Make of It:

Each of us has our own understanding of money. For some, money means freedom, while for others it spells power, respectability, or success. Money can be the way that we prove ourselves worthy—to our friends, our families, and maybe even to ourselves.

If money is a lousy boss but a good servant, what values do you associate with it?

— While I was growing up, money meant . . .

— Now, money means . . .

— The money I earn allows me to . . .

— If I was earning substantially more than I am now I'd be free to . . .

## THE GREENBACK BLUES

The major complaint that people have about their jobs is that they don't make enough money. Sometimes, this is the result of their own poor budgeting. It may be the result of difficult circumstances, a failing economy, or of the individual's own deliberate choice to value other things more highly than income. And sometimes dissatisfaction is the result of one of the attitudes about money that we examined above.

It may be helpful to distinguish a number of different meanings of the phrase, "I'm not making enough money." If you feel this way about your own situation, ask yourself which of the following categories you fall into:

— Overall, I'm very happy with the work I do. I genuinely enjoy it, and I've made my peace with the fact that it doesn't pay very well. But when it comes to asking the rest of my family to share this attitude, I begin to wonder whether I'm being fair to them. I just don't seem to be making enough money . . .

— My income is fair compared to what others around me are paid. I've been pretty successful and received a number of raises. But it is beginning to look as though no increase is large enough to allow me to live within my budget. What it boils down to is that the costs of living—the clothes for the job, the kids' needs, the new house—rise every time I get a raise. I don't make enough money . . .

— I'm just not being paid fairly for what I do, and I'm not getting the promotions I deserve. The man in the same job next to me, on the other hand . . .

— My income is so small compared to my wants that my life feels pinched, and I see no end in sight. I may not be in debt, but I don't feel very much enthusiasm about the future. I'm just not making enough money . . .

— I spend money to feel a happiness that, deep down, I just don't feel much of the time. I find that I'm happy enough while I'm actually spending money, but the things I buy stop making me happy almost as soon as I've gotten them home . . .

— I'm paid enough to cover my expenses, and even do many of the things I'd like to do. But I figure I am worth more than I presently receive, and that makes me kind of mad. I know I'm not being paid as much as I'm worth . . .

Does one of these examples describe your situation? If it does, you may want to explore the possibility of striking a different balance between the money you earn and the trade-offs you're prepared to make to earn it.

## ABUNDANT SIMPLICITY

Take a look at two attitudes toward money that have become increasingly popular over the last few years. Each one offers a means of shifting that balance in a direction that increases your satisfaction with the pay your receive for the work you do.

• Abundance Consciousness:

Abundance consciousness is the idea that you have the right to a life of abundance. Certainly, nature is bountiful, and at least until Columbus arrived, there were more than enough cranberries and turkeys to go around. The idea is that we live in a creation that naturally supplies us with abundance, and that only the fear that we don't deserve abundance can hold it back from us. For people who feel undeserving, it's an idea that can have a profoundly beneficial effect.

Abundance consciousness stems from the basic understanding that we all have a great deal more to do with the way our lives turn out than we admit. In some sense, each one of us writes the script for our own life. The personal dramas we find unfolding in our lives are often the ones we have quietly chosen. When you recognize this fact, something remarkable can happen. You come to realize that you can change your script. And these changes can make the difference between feeling victimized and feeling on top of things.

"There is more victim-consciousness attached to money than just about anything else," Terry Cole-Whittaker suggests in her book, *How to Have More in a Have Not World.* "Money victims are everywhere, and they aren't limited to just the poor. The very rich can also be victims of the money game. Those who are money victims blame a lot. They blame those with money, they blame their kids for being a burden to them, they blame their mates for spending too much or not earning enough; they blame the government, their employers, even their astrological signs."

Many people, if they examine their lives carefully, realize that they have some self-defeating patterns. They regularly set themselves up to fail, at a tennis return, a diet, or a job interview. It's important to start taking credit for personal failures, as well as successes.

If your life feels pinched because of financial insufficiency, you may want to ask yourself whether any of your patterns relating to money are self-defeating.

— Do you have attitudes about money that you would like to change? What about attitudes that may be holding you back from making more money?

— When you have more money than usual, do you have patterns of spending it that bring you little satisfaction?

— Do you ever refuse yourself the chance to get satisfaction from spending relatively small sums of money?

Prosperity, according to bumper stickers we've seen, is your divine right. But this notion of prosperity raises some profound questions about the nature of the world we live in, as well as about your own attitudes to money. Is it true that the resources of the planet are finite? That as the rich get richer, the poor get poorer? If so, is that a price you want to pay for abundance? It sometimes seems as if abundance consciousness comes uncomfortably close to Janis Joplin's classic line, "O Lord, won't you buy me a Mercedes Benz." Is keeping up with the Porsches what divine providence is all about?

- Voluntary Simplicity:

"Small is beautiful" is a phrase coined by the economist, E.F. Schumacher, to emphasize that the massive technology of the Western world may not be the most appropriate technology in all cases. It also suggests that we live on a small planet with limited resources. As J. Edwin Matz, president of John Hancock Mutual Life Insurance Company puts it, "Somehow one feels that ultimately there must be a better solution, that there needs to be a state of economic well-being which does not depend on an ever increasing number of people exploiting the finite resources of the planet at an ever accelerating rate." The other side of the coin from abundance, if you like, is scarcity.

A number of people are working out ways to live in what they call "voluntary simplicity." They are streamlining their lives to get as much satisfaction as possible from simple things —a walk in the woods, or exploring local architecture—and from using their abilities—fixing their own car or planting their own vegetables.

"To bring the quality of simplicity into our levels and patterns of consumption," writes Duane Elgin in his book, *Voluntary Simplicity,* "we must learn to live between the extremes of poverty and excess. Simplicity is a double-edged sword in this regard: living with either too little or with too much will diminish our capacity to realize our human potentials. Bringing simplicity into our lives thus requires that we understand the ways in which our consumption either supports or entangles our existence . . . Simplicity requires living with balance."

"The rich man is the man who is satisfied with what he has," says the *Talmud*. One very simple strategy for dealing with "not being paid enough" is to see whether you can be happy with less. Don't knock this idea without giving it a fair hearing. Compulsive spenders understand only too well Wordsworth's remark, "Getting and spending, we lay waste our powers." They know just how easy it is to run up impossible bills on charge accounts in an effort to buy that very elusive quality, happiness.

Both the practitioners of voluntary simplicity and those who are trying to stop spending money compulsively are finding ways to do more with less. They are enjoying a shift in attitude that brings out unexpected strengths and skills, and ultimately brings unexpected joy to their lives. "I'm more self-reliant" is the way they often express it.

Let's take a closer look at the idea of enjoying more while spending less. One senior executive we spoke with told us that he recently spent thousands of dollars for a family vacation abroad. What intrigued him most was that he admitted he'd received as much genuine pleasure from reading a five dollar paperback he'd picked up at the airport as he had on the actual trip.

"It's not that the trip wasn't fun," he told us, "it's just that I got as much from the book as I got from sitting on the white sandy beach."

We are so accustomed to the idea that inexpensive things can't be "worth" much, that we sometimes ignore simple pleasures and exaggerate the benefits of expensive ones.

— What actually brings you the greatest delight?

— Are some of your real pleasures pretty inexpensive?

— What are some of your more expensive pleasures?

— Are there times when you'd actually find greater satisfaction by foregoing one of your more expensive pleasures, and enjoying some of the less expensive ones instead?

— Could you have more with less?

Voluntary simplicity and abundance consciousness are both ways to approach situations where you find your earnings don't match up to your expenses. You can increase the amount you earn, and abundance consciousness may help you. Or you can change your attitude to enjoy the sense of internal abundance that comes with voluntary simplicity. You may even decide you want to try both, and work out your own individual fusion between these two styles. Although they may seem at first to contradict one another, they don't have to. They often need to work together if they are to work at all.

## THE GREAT TRADE-OFF

Is the time you put in at work a good trade-off for what the money you earn buys you?

People tell themselves that money is worth almost anything they might have to do to get it, and all too often that includes working at a job that really doesn't satisfy them. Indeed, this idea is so much a part of our culture that to question it seems nearly unthinkable. It's usually worth probing around a bit, though, when you run into one of those "unquestionable" assumptions. They tend to hide important truths.

The logic of the "trade-off" assumption is often expressed like this: "You can either go for the money, or go for the job you'd really prefer. I choose the money, because I'll be able to afford the kind of life I want to lead." That's a reasonable hypothesis, but like all hypotheses, it needs to be tested against the facts.

— Does the money you earn in fact buy you the life you want?

— When you think about it carefully, are you satisfied with what your money brings you?

— How much are you willing to give up in return for the money you earn? How much time? How much energy? Where would you draw the line?

— How successful is the trade-off you're currently making? Could it be improved? What would the optimal balance look like?

These are questions that you need to weigh for yourself, and you should carry them with you while you're going through the rest of this book. Everything you do to make your work more enjoyable will tend to tilt the balance further in your favor. At the same time, anything you can do to reduce your financial needs will also help you swing the balance. The less money you require, the greater freedom you'll have to choose the kind of work that's deeply satisfying.

Attitudes toward money have begun to change. Recent studies conducted by Yankelovich, Skelly, and White reveal that 75 percent of Americans no longer find the prospect of working at a boring job "as long as the pay is good" acceptable, and 78 percent say they would refuse to leave a job they liked for one that paid more.

As you come to the end of this chapter, you should take a moment to clarify and summarize what you've learned about your attitudes toward money. What does money mean to you? How do your attitudes influence your financial situation? What have you learned about yourself from this chapter? And above all, is the time you spend at work a good trade-off?

Now wind up with a few more sentence completion exercises:

— When the going gets rough financially, I often feel . . .

— My overly pragmatic attitude to money sometimes prevents me from . . .

— My overly idealistic approach to money sometimes keeps me from . . .

— A balanced approach to money would allow me to . . .

— I'm beginning to see that when it comes to money . . .

## THE PRICE OF FREEDOM

Before we leave the subject of money and turn to the other aspects of work satisfaction, there are two warnings we'd like to repeat.

The first warning goes like this: there is little freedom in working only for money. This wouldn't be a very important warning if so many of us didn't allow money to overinfluence the way we make decisions.

The second warning is even simpler. It applies to anyone who tends to let their idealism drive them into impossible corners. It is this: there is very little freedom in poverty.

# INDIVIDUAL SATISFACTION

**Relevance:** This chapter is for those who feel their present job doesn't entirely suit their skills, preferences, and personality.

**Premise:** The second level of work satisfaction is achieved when the work you do is suited to your tastes, and makes use of and develops your talents.

**Strategy:** Explore your skills and aptitudes, your passions and delights, and see how they can be applied to your work.

**Tactics:** Keep track of which activities leave you feeling energized and up; research your skills; explore what jobs are currently available, and what changes are to be expected in the job market of the future.

# Chapter 4

---

# INDIVIDUAL SATISFACTION

*To business that we love we rise betime,*
*And go to't with delight.*

*William Shakespeare*

No two people are the same.

Some people love taking things apart and putting them back together; all other things being equal, they'd prefer work that used that gift. Some people love talking with other people, but have never managed to put anything back together, although they've taken things apart from time to time.

Suppose you're one of the takers-apart and putters-together. And let's suppose you also have a passion for films, and are a somewhat private and ornery individual, who likes to work late hours and sleep in. Working as a cinema projectionist might be a dream job for you; it would both fit your skills and suit your preferences.

Then again, if you're the sort of person who gets up at sunrise and likes the open air, movie-projecting would probably turn out to be a nightmare even if the pay was great. But working as a fire lookout might suit you fine.

This chapter is about those kinds of differences, and what they mean in terms of job satisfaction.

# THE JOB THAT'S WRITTEN IN YOUR STARS

Some people have a very clear sense of what they are cut out to do. It is as though the instructions for their entire lives were somehow written into their DNA—"it was written in his genes" is another way of saying "it was written in the stars."

Some of these people seem to have arrived at birth with a little black bag in one hand and a stethoscope in the other. Going to medical school was not so much a choice as a foregone conclusion. When they graduated, they quickly discovered that sick people felt naturally comforted by them. Years of medical training translated into a sort of intuition, the intuition into diagnosis, the diagnosis into treatment—and from there on, they were what we sometimes call "born doctors."

We talk about born doctors, born teachers, maybe even born architects or engineers. They have what used to be known as a vocation, a calling. But how about born plumbers? Born secretaries? Born dental hygienists? Born insurance brokers? The fact is that many people don't feel as though they are "born" anythings. They are good at some things, and not so interested in others, but that's about as far as it goes.

It is time to propose a redefinition of the word "vocation" so that everyone can see more possibilities in life. We need to stop limiting the use of this word to a few specialized professions, and open it up to include any kind of work that expresses a person's skills and preferences. It is possible for you to find the work (and probably even the job) that you have a flair for, that you can delight in, and that makes full use of your skills and talents—to uncover your own vocation.

# FOCUSING ON YOUR PREFERENCES

The approach here will be different from, though complementary to, the approach focusing on skills and aptitudes that you will find elsewhere. It's time to ask yourself some questions that will emphasize your preferences and delights rather than your skills.

Many people have developed skills that they don't particularly enjoy. They learned the job their parents wanted them to learn, or which was available at the time, and now they are looking for a greater sense of meaning and accomplishment. And interest, rather than skill, is the first criterion for the kind of work that brings you the second level of satisfaction. The business of identifying satisfying work is largely a business of self-discovery and self-expression.

Tom Drucker, who was the head of management training for Xerox, and now runs his own consulting firm, explains things this way: "Some time ago, the work people did was generally isolated from their passions, values, and beliefs. Then came the "Age of Entitlement," when both employees and employers began to feel that employees were entitled to work satisfaction. It was largely a matter of getting these two areas to overlap.

"The best of recent management theory suggests that it's the worker's responsibility to see that that overlap takes place, and that's just as well. Nobody wants their employer to decide what their passions, values, and beliefs should be."

- Passion and Delight:

What do you really enjoy doing? What is your delight? Your passion? These are the key questions. If you do what delights you, you're well-satisfied.

The problem, though, is to know what does delight you. And it can be even harder to know when a multitude of thoughts about job descriptions, money, and prestige are whizzing around in your brain. Many people simply don't allow themselves to consider their own delights because at best they seem tangential to the search for satisfying work, and at worst simply frivolous. In fact, they are crucial.

As you begin to think about these questions, bear in mind that the answers you give may not translate directly into job descriptions. If your answers suggest obvious kinds of work, well and good. If not, don't worry. Keep focusing on what you enjoy, and you will begin to discover some of the key components of the kind of work you need to find.

Use the following sentence completions as a way to explore your delights and preferences:

— If I had a bumper sticker, it would read "I'd rather be . . ."

— One thing I really enjoy about my present work is . . .

— I lose track of time when I . . .

Now focus in on those specific accomplishments and skills that have brought you pleasure. Feel free to chose whichever sentence completions work best for you, and remember to fill in the sentences you choose several times each.

— One thing I do really well is . . .

— One accomplishment that really delighted me was . . .

— One skill I enjoy using is . . .

— I'm fascinated by . . .

— One skill I'd love to learn is . . .

Now take your answers and push them further. Fill in the first blank in the next few sentences with the answers you gave above, and allow yourself to go into more detail about what it is that delights you.

— The thing I enjoy most about . . . is . . .

— I enjoy . . . because . . .

— The thing I'd enjoy most about learning . . . is . . .

You can do the same thing with the sentence completions above which seemed to have most meaning for you.

— What have you learned so far about the things that really delight you, and the way these fit into the work you do?

One of the ways to get a closer fix on these things is to watch for the "symptoms" of delight. Here are a variety of clues to the things that "make you come alive."

• Increased Energy:

Feeling alert and energetic is one of the "symptoms" of really enjoying what you are doing. In fact, when we are enjoying things the most, we may be too busy to notice just how good we feel. If your mind drew something of a blank as you were going through the "delight" section, take a look at these "symptoms."

Make a list of the activities that leave you with plenty of energy. Of course some of the things we enjoy most, particularly if we work outdoors, may leave us pleasantly exhausted—but that's very different from being drained.

— The best moments in my working week are . . .

— One part of my work that really keeps me alert is . . .

— I get a pleasant feeling of exhaustion when I have . . .

— One aspect of my work (or work that I have done in the past) that leaves me feeling energized is . . .

• Enthusiasm:

Everyone probably has some idea of what their real passions and enthusiasms are, yet people often tend to downplay them because they "just don't see themselves that way" when they think about earning a living. For instance, perhaps you love to garden, but it may not have occurred to you to consider whether that interest could be a part of your work. Yet you need to acknowledge your passions if you are to find the work that will satisfy you the most. Your own enthusiasm is probably one of the most valuable qualities that you bring to your work, from your employer's point of view as well as your own.

- Talking up a Storm:

Another "symptom" of real passion is that you can't stop talking it. Ask yourself which aspects of your work you talk most enthusiastically about in your daily conversations with other people. You'll be pinpointing the areas of your work that mean the most to you, and you may realize that your present work gives you more (or less) satisfaction than you thought.

Michael's story is an example of this. He currently works in the executive end of publishing. He was recently talking with a psychologist friend who told him, "When I talk to other people in publishing, Mike, they generally tell me about their firm's next best-seller and how much money it's going to make. They tell me about their colleagues, the industry, the new procedures they are thinking about implementing, and so on. When I talk to you, all I hear about is the content of the newest book you're working on. You seem to think that promotion and marketing are only there to get the book's ideas as widely distributed as possible, not to sell copies."

Michael is often discontented with his work, because he spends a good part of his week involved with questions of sales potential, financing, and promotion. It surprised him to find out how important a book's content is to him, and how little his actual work reflects his real enthusiasm. If the ideas in a book are what mean the most to Michael, as he ruefully remarked to us, perhaps he'd be better off making less money and working for a university press, rather than a commercially oriented firm.

— When I talk about my work, the part that I like and tend to dwell on is . . .

— My friends notice the pride in my voice when I mention . . .

— To hear me tell it, you'd think my work was all . . .

— I'd enjoy my work more if it involved less. . . . and more . . .

Michael's story brings up another way to tell what your real enthusiasms are: by watching the way you make use of your time, and comparing that with the use you would like to make of it. Make up a pie chart with different-sized slices that correspond to the amounts of time you put into different activities in the course of an average day: work, travel, and free time. Next, divide up your "work" slice and your "free time" slice into smaller slices that correspond to specific activities.

How much of your working day is spent in activities that you enjoy? That you can't stand? That are neutral? How about your free time?

Now make up a second pie chart that shows how you would prefer to divide your time. What do your pie charts show you about your enthusiasms, and the degree to which you find time for them? Could you "bake yourself a better pie" by finding more time to express your interests and delights in your work, or by finding work that expresses more of those interests and delights?

● Giving Your Right Arm:

Ian's first job was at a TV station. You couldn't keep him away from the place. He was there at 8:00 AM, and although his job was officially over at 5:00 PM, he would hang around the station several evenings a week, helping out with shows he wasn't responsible for, and puttering back to his office from time to time to see what he could do to prepare for the next day's work.

We have to admit that Ian was single at the time, but his attitude is not uncommon among people whose work genuinely fascinates them. Some people—artists, athletes, computer whizzes—would almost pay to do the things they are paid to do. What aspects of your work could you feel that way about? Pull together what you've learned about your passions, and put it into the context of work.

— I'd happily work overtime if I could . . .

— I'd work for free if the work involved . . .

— I'd maybe even pay to be allowed to . . .

- Learning and Growth:

The sense that you are learning something, or growing as a human being, is another one of the "symptoms" by which you can recognize real enthusiasm. More will be said about this in Chapter Eight, which is concerned with learning as a step toward optimal employment. For now, let's just say that learning and growth are two of the key factors in finding satisfaction in your work.

Once again, summarize your findings with a few sentence completions.

— The work I do allows me to discover more about . . .

— I learn most from my work when I am . . .

— I'd enjoy work that allowed me to learn . . .

— The work I have done has helped me to grow more in terms of . . .

— The aspect of work that contributes most to my growth is . . .

- Flair:

Lastly, each one of us has certain things that we do with flair. They seem effortless, and we do them gracefully, masterfully. Sometimes we discover ourselves going into a kind of "overdrive" that allows us to get an amazing amount of work accomplished in a short time because we're able to sidestep our usual doubts and hesitations.

To summarize,

— One aspect of my work that runs like clockwork is . . .

— There's an effortless quality to the times when I . . .

— People tell me I have a flair for . . .

— Sometimes I feel like a master of . . .

Work that you can feel passionate about, that engages your interest, and expresses your deepest values, is likely to be work that involves using your passions, interests, and values on a day-to-day basis. That's where satisfaction lies.

## SKILLS AND APTITUDES

There are various ways to go about the business of assessing your skills. Your job physical contained a skills questionnaire, and we'd like you now to go back and read the notes you took. This time, pay special attention to the ways in which your skills tie in with the topics just discussed. Note the skills you possess that contribute to your delight, energy, enthusiasm, and flair.

- Aptitude Tests:

If you want to delve into the subject of skills more deeply, one way to go about it is to take a test. Many personnel agencies and school placement offices offer batteries of questionnaires that are designed to probe your skills and aptitudes. There are two major benefits to taking an aptitude test, and there's also a drawback.

The first benefit is that they put you in contact with someone whose profession it is to draw you out on the subject of your skills, interests, and dreams—and to know enough about the job market to help you see where those skills might be used. Employment counselors may also use their own network of personnel managers and previous clients to put you in touch with a job.

The other advantage to testing is that a trained job counselor may be able to see things about you that you can't recognize on your own. Information about skills and jobs is valuable, but insight into yourself is priceless. This is where you can benefit the most, but it's also where the problem can arise. Someone who is trained to recognize different types of skills and aptitudes, but who is not you, is going to advise you about your career. If you simply take their advice without reflection, you are trusting yourself to someone else's best judgment.

The best approach to aptitude tests is to let them clarify as much as they can for you, and then put them into perspective yourself. Take an active role in the process. Find a counselor you feel comfortable with, and explore your potential with him or her. A good tester will understand if you want to approach job counseling this way. They're not there to make infallible pronouncements, but to help you find work that's rewarding in both senses of the word. In the final analysis it's your life, and you need to be at the controls.

● Parachute:

There's another way that you can track down your skills and aptitudes in more detail. Richard Bolles' delightful book, *What Color Is Your Parachute?*, is far and away the best "skills-inventory" book on the market.

*Parachute* contains a wealth of information about the way to go about looking for a job, and proposes that the orthodox route via advertisement and resume is far from optimal. If you come to the conclusion that you know the kind of work that would really satisfy you, and want to go out into the marketplace and find it, Bolles' book is the best handbook you could want.

In the meantime, consider the theory proposed by John L. Holland and stated in *Parachute* by Bolles concerning the six main categories of human groups and the kind of work they do based on their predominate skills.

— The first group of people are those who like to work with things. They are the fixers (of complex mechanisms), the growers (of plants and animals), the engineers, the technologists.

— Group two contains those who like to work with data; people with numerical or clerical abilities. This group is well suited to work in areas that demand a fine attention to detail: accounting, business management, computer programming.

— Group three includes people who like to influence others: salesmen and managers, people in real estate, industrial relations, public administration, lawyers, diplomats.

— People in group four like working in service professions: educators, health professionals, personnel managers.

— The fifth group is interested in innovation and intuition. These are the people who make creative breakthroughs, the artists, musicians, designers, and philosophers among us.

— Finally, the people in group six are investigative and analytic by nature. They like to solve problems. Chemical engineers, psychologists, systems analysts, and medical researchers will recognize themselves in this group.

Which group comes closest to describing you? Is the work you currently do (or the work you're thinking of doing) appropriate for someone of your temperament?

Another important section of *Parachute* is called "The Quick Job-Hunting Map." It contains some fascinating statistics, such as that on the average, employers make one job-offer for every 1,470 resumes they receive. It includes an exercise that discusses the six skills types. And it ends with an extremely detailed skills inventory.

## MATTERS OF LIFE AND DEATH

You have explored your preferences, enthusiasms, passions, and skills in the context of real time work—the work you actually do, or the work you might like to be doing. Now let's up the ante a little, throw caution to the winds, push the limits of reality, and get down to business. The next three sets of sentence completions go together. Each of them deals with an extreme situation, and offers you an opportunity to take your understanding of yourself and your work to a deeper level.

- Curtains:

Suppose you only had a short time left to live, and you knew it. What would you feel was worth doing? Your answers to this question can tell you a lot about where your values lie.

— If I only had a year to live, I'd like to . . .

— The most valuable thing of all that I could do would be . . .

— If it's the last thing on earth I do, I'll . . .

- The Fountain of Youth:

You may not even think about attempting the things you'd most enjoy doing, because you imagine they would take too long to accomplish. It's important to think about them, however, because they contain clues to your nature, your personality, and preferences. Even if that clue isn't enough by itself to define a possible job, it may be when it's woven into the larger fabric of your self-understanding.

Some of your dreams may actually be perfectly possible. Many people don't do the work they'd really like to do because they think they're too old, or perhaps they worry that the economy will change before they finish the training.

- — If I knew I had all the time in the world, I'd begin at once with . . .

- — I'd learn everything there is to know about . . .

- — I'd take the time to learn how to . . .

- The Inexhaustible Uncle:

This question is designed to get beyond the things we do for money, and take a closer look at the things we'd like to do for their own sake. Suppose that all your concerns about material well-being were taken care of, and that you had an inexhaustibly wealthy and indulgent uncle who would provide you with unlimited funds for the rest of your life. What would you like to do with your time?

- — If I had all the money I could use, I'd spend my days . . .

- — I'd feel free to . . .

- — I'd become involved in . . .

- — Nothing would keep me from . . .

These three sets of questions have allowed you to focus on some deeply important aspects of your life. If you can tailor your work to reflect these understandings, your job will mean more to you, absorb you more fully, and offer you a deeper level of satisfaction. Now you need to wrap up with a few completions that gather in what you've learned.

— I'm learning that what really matters to me is . . .

— I've known all along that what really stimulates me is . . .

— I'm beginning to see my work needs to . . .

## WHEN YOU'VE MISPLACED YOUR DREAM

Shirley has devoted most of her life to raising three children, all of whom are now in school. She has reached a point where she recognizes that it's time for a change, but she doesn't know what direction to move in. She feels as though there's nothing that really interests her. She wasn't able to come up with a single thing that she'd want to do, whether it was her last chance on earth, or if she could live forever, or was fabulously wealthy. When she read through those last three questions, she didn't know how to answer; she just sat and quietly cried for fifteen minutes.

If you're in a similar situation, what other options do you have? One solution to your problem may lie in knowing more about the kinds of work that do exist. Finding out about a wide variety of available jobs is certainly one way to widen the scope of your search.

Even if you have a clear sense of your skills, talents, and dreams, learning more about the kinds of work that are available can be a necessary and stimulating part of your self-discovery. Your talents are the wine; the world of work is the glass into which those talents can be poured.

In the rest of this chapter we shall examine the ways in which you can find out what jobs do exist that might spark your enthusiasm and utilize your skills. We will take a look at the ways in which the workplace can be expected to change over the next ten or twenty years.

• Invisible Jobs:

Most jobs are invisible. That is to say that there are many more jobs out there than anyone can possibly imagine. You may find out about certain jobs because someone you know does them, or because you've read about them or seen them on TV. But do you personally know anyone who designs greetings cards or hospital furniture? Makes golfballs or sings telegrams? Breeds new varieties of roses or new strains of tea? Works on the restoration of old pictures? Somebody, somewhere, does.

How can you find out what jobs there are that you don't even know exist? You might want to take a look at Jonathan Price's book, *How to Find Work.* It lists more than 300 job descriptions. These are taken from a U.S. Department of Labor catalogue, *The Dictionary of Occupational Titles* (DOT), which contains 20,000 job descriptions. Your public library probably has a copy of this massive publication. A sample entry looks like this:

FIRE LOOKOUT: Locates and reports forest fires and weather phenomena from remote fire-lookout station. Maintains surveillance from station to detect evidence of fires and observe weather conditions. Locates fires on area map, using azimuth sighter and known landmarks, estimates size and characteristics of fire, and reports findings to base camp by radio or telephone. Observes instruments and reports daily meteorological data, such as temperature, relative humidity, wind direction and velocity, and type of cloud formations. Relays messages from base camp, mobile units, and law enforcement and government agencies relating to weather forecasts, fire hazard conditions, emergencies, accidents, and location of crews and personnel. Explains state and federal laws, timber company policies, fire hazard conditions, and fire prevention methods to visitors of forest. Maintains records and logbooks. (367)

Or this:

ART THERAPIST: Plans and conducts art therapy programs in public and private institutions to rehabilitate mentally ill and physically disabled patients: Confers with members of medically oriented team to determine nature of patient illness. Recommends art therapy program for patients. Devises program and instructs patients in art techniques. Encourages and guides patient participation. Appraises patients' art projects and recovery progress. Reports findings to other members of treatment team and counsels on patient's response until art therapy is discontinued. Maintains and repairs art materials and equipment. (127)

Or this:

SILK-SCREEN PRINTER: Tends silk-screen machine that prints designs or lettering on glassware, pottery, and metal and plastic items, such as appliances, instrument dials, and toys. Bolts framed silk-screen onto machine, and installs and adjusts workpiece holding fixture, stops, and guides, using handtools, ruler, and workpiece pattern. Attaches squeegee to pneumatic drive mechanism, using wrench, and couples air line to mechanism. Regulates air pressure and manipulates squeegee to adjust squeegee pressure and angle of sweep. Applies printing compound to screen, using spatula or brush. Places workpiece in or on holding fixture, presses button to lower screen, and depresses pedal or pushes button to activate squeegee. Observes silk-screen and workpiece to detect printing defects caused by rip in screen and applies glue to repair screen. Cleans silk-screen, using brush and solvent. May thin printing compound, using specified thinner. May tend firing oven to dry printed workpiece (665).

Or this:

MOTION-PICTURE PROJECTIONIST: Sets up and operates motion picture projection and sound-reproducing equipment to produce coordinated effects on screen. Inserts film into top magazine reel of projector. Threads film through picture aperture of projector, around pressure rollers, sprocket wheels, and sound drum or magnetic sound pickup on film, and onto spool that automatically takes up film slack. Regulates projection light and adjusts sound-reproducing equipment. Monitors operation of machines and transfers operation from one machine to another without interrupting flow of action on screen. Rewinds broken end of film onto reels by hand to minimize loss of time. Inspects and rewinds projected films for another showing. Repairs faulty sections of film. Operates stereopticon (magic lantern) or other special-effects equipment to project picture slides on screen. Cleans lenses, oils equipment, and makes minor repairs and adjustments. (362)

Simply glancing through 300 (or 20,000) titles may remind you of the existence of many jobs that you wouldn't ordinarily recall. But what more can you learn from specific entries?

The first thing to notice is the three-digit code at the end of each listing. In the case of the fire lookout, this read (367).

These codes follow government standards for job descriptions, and rate necessary skills in three areas: data, people, and things. Notice how these categories correspond to the six types of skills that Bolles noted in *Parachute*.

Low numbers on this government scale (1–3) imply that high-quality skills are required in this area. Conversely, high numbers (7–9) imply a lower level of skill. (If this numbering system sounds backward, remember it's the way the government has chosen to label these things.)

From the 367 code for fire lookouts, we learn that overall, the job requires a fairly high level of skill (3) in handling data (ideas and information in word or image); lesser skills (6) in dealing with people; and even less skill (7) in dealing with things (machines, equipment, products, and tools).

What else do we learn? That fire lookouts frequently work in remote locations, particularly forests. That their job requires them to use equipment (azimuth sighters, radio) and make clear and detailed reports of natural phenomena (maintain surveillance and report findings). And they need skills in the area of interacting smoothly but firmly with other people (to explain laws, policies, fire hazard conditions, and fire prevention methods).

We might also guess from this listing that the position is ideal for people who like their work to make a contribution to society, who enjoy the outdoors, and who are happy to spend considerable amounts of time with relatively little social interaction.

From the (217) code for Art Therapists, we learned that the job involved a high level of skill (2) in handling people, as well as data (1), and relatively little skill (7) with things. Let's rephrase that a little less technically and more humanely, by reading between the lines. It's a job that requires both a real sense of caring for people, and an enjoyment of creativity. That's a powerful and rewarding combination, if it fits your bill.

The Silk-Screen listing suggests a job that makes relatively little demand on any of the three types of skills (665), and we might deduce from the description that the job involves technical competence at a largely routine task.

Similarly, the listing for Projectionists tells us that the job involves some manual dexterity (all those sprockets and rollers), and that it requires some technical skill (minor repairs and adjustments).

It doesn't tell us, though we might well imagine (or find out from a friend) that a projectionist works strange hours, cut off from the outside world in a small booth that nobody much visits, where he or she is free to watch movies, but more likely, perhaps, to read *War and Peace* during the twelfth screening of *Revenge of the Barbershop Vampires,* and that eccentrics delight in the Howard Hughes isolation of the job.

The information in these listings, then, describes the tasks technically, and gives relatively little direct insight into the types of people that might enjoy each occupation. The listings can provide you with new ideas, but to get a complete picture you need to talk with the people who actually do the kinds of work you think might interest you.

● A Glance into the Future:

Another way to open up your thinking about jobs is to take a look into the future. What if your natural gifts and abilities suit you for work which does not yet exist? If Mozart could be a musical genius at the age of six, isn't it possible that some of us were born "video geniuses," going through school at a time when no one understood how big the video industry would become?

Are you a keen science fiction reader? When the day's work is over, do you rush into the future with John Brunner's *Shockwave Rider* or Samuel Delany's *Rydra Wong*? Do you belong to the L-5 society, and hope to transfer to a space colony? Is your favorite instrument the synthesizer? Were you born to play computer games? Some people are waiting impatiently for the twenty-first century to begin.

As David Borchard, president of Middle Atlantic Career Counseling Association, remarked in a recent article in *The Futurist,* "One of the major problems confronting the neophyte career/life-planning professional is the pace at which the occupational world is now changing. Many of the specific career-related programs that college freshmen and technical-school students enter into today may no longer offer good employment prospects or long-range career potential by the time they obtain their degrees."

Borchard goes on to suggest two kinds of change that may come about over the next few years, the seeds of which are already present in our culture. He says we may expect to see either "rapid change in human creations, such as technology, economics and politics, with little change in humans themselves," or "rapid change in humans, such as brain/mind capabilities, health, and values."

In other words, the sorts of work that are available may change as our world becomes ever more technologically sophisticated. Or the sorts of values people have with regard to their work may change as people delve deeper into themselves and their motivations. Or possibly both.

• The Future of Work:

In the fifteen essays collected in *Work in the 21st Century,* published by the American Society for Personnel Administration, a number of writers, Daniel Yankelovich and Isaac Asimov among them, take a look at the changing face of work.

Basing his assessment on the results of a three-year international research project entitled "Jobs in the 1980s and 1990s," Yankelovich suggests that "the workplace will be primarily characterized by high-discretion jobs, where individual jobholders have a great deal of latitude over how they perform their work," and that "a much larger proportion" of jobholders will see themselves as "primarily working to fulfill their expressive needs."

Isaac Asimov foresees a world in which much of the "grindwork" will be done by robots and computers, and in which leisure occupations will play a much greater role than at present. He predicts that as a result, show business, sports, and the arts will grow steadily more important.

But it is the list of "emerging careers" suggested by Dr. Norman Feingold, president of National Career and Counseling Services of Washington, that most clearly brings home the scope of the changes we can look forward to. Among the careers he lists are: asteroid miner, genetic counselor, hibernation specialist, underwater hotel director, and wind prospector.

Imagine what the government *DOT* listing will make of jobs like these:

WIND PROSPECTOR: Analyzes and interprets meteorological data gathered by surface and upper-air stations, satellites, and radar to prepare suitability reports for public and private clients. Studies wind flow patterns for optimal energy entrapment. Consults with clients on available forms of wind technology, including light alloy windmills and wind/solar combinations. May conduct basic or applied research. (052)

Better yet, choose your own ideal futuristic job, and write up a *DOT* listing for it.

Of course, many jobs that are already familiar to us will also exist in the foreseeable future. A recent article by Robin Warshaw in a special campus edition of *MS.* magazine ranked future jobs for college graduates into four categories.

"Surefire Hits" are those jobs that Warshaw predicts will increase rapidly by the 1990s, and where there will be little competition for openings. They include computer systems analysts and programmers, health service administrators, occupational and physical therapists.

"Growth Jobs," which include aerospace, civil, chemical, industrial, metallurgical, and nuclear engineers, accountants, and preschool and elementary teachers, will also increase to some extent, although competition for jobs will be somewhat stronger in these areas.

Actors, designers, architects, stockbrokers, writers, physicians, lawyers, and real estate agents are listed under the heading "The Combat Zone." Warshaw predicts that openings in these areas will increase to some extent, but will be highly competitive.

And listed under "The Impossible Dream," are jobs where the numbers of openings are expected to remain the same or decline, and where "very stiff competition" is to be expected: public relations, economists, dentists, social workers.

Of course the future is unpredictable, and these lists may seem quaint and outdated when the twenty-first century rolls around. At best, they offer you an inspired guess at what the future may look like, as well as suggesting some possible job categories for you to think over and research. Once again, these listings are only useful to the degree that they "click" with your own sense of what you as an individual would really like to do.

Information is the currency of the future. In terms of finding satisfying work, that doesn't simply mean that jobs in the "information industry" are going to be at a premium. It also implies that the amount of information you have about yourself and the kinds of work available will largely determine the choices you will be able to make.

Ask yourself how informed you are about the job market, and about the major trends and shifts in our society. Do you know as much as you would like to about the breadth and variety of the jobs "out there," or the ways in which work itself may change over the next two or three decades? If not, it's worth scheduling a visit to the reference room at your local library. Give yourself at least a couple hours. Use the *DOT* or pick up copies of Bolles' and Price's books. Read science fiction or future fact.

Talk about jobs. Talk about the future. Make a point of finding out what other people do, and how they feel about it. When you run across a job description or trend that sounds interesting, note it down with a few basic facts. Don't worry about whether you possess particular qualifications or not, just jot down some of the details. Simply becoming more aware of what's going on in the work world around you is liable to open up a variety of possibilities.

# SATISFACTION PLUS

**Relevance:** This chapter is for those who wish to give of themselves to others.

**Premise:** The deepest kinds of satisfaction that work can offer come from giving of oneself.

**Strategy:** By making your work a contribution to those around you, or by doing work that expresses your potential to a marked, even inspired, degree, you can experience satisfaction plus.

**Tactics:** Finding your vocation; discovering areas where "something must be done" and doing it; and exploring mythology and archetypal vocations.

# Chapter 5

# SATISFACTION PLUS

*Far and away the best prize that life offers is the chance to work hard at work worth doing.*

*Theodore Roosevelt*

You have looked at the first level of work satisfaction, covering your financial requirements, and explored the second, finding work that you honestly enjoy. But there is a third level which grows naturally out of the second. The distinctions between them may be hard to define, but in its upper reaches, the third level is quite distinct.

For some, this is the level of satisfaction which comes from making a contribution to the world around them. For others, it is the joy of expressing their own gifts and talents at an inspired level. In both cases, the satisfaction comes from moving beyond oneself and one's personal concerns to the satisfaction of giving.

Psychologist Abraham Maslow, after investigating the lives of people who enjoy an exceptional sense of well-being, pointed out that people seem to possess what he called a "hierarchy of needs." Thus the desperately hungry will search for food with little concern for their own safety. Once hunger, thirst, and the need for sleep are satisfied, then safety and security become the paramount concerns, and so on up the ladder through the need for love and esteem. The final motive, which Maslow found people responded to when all else was taken care of, he called the need for self-actualization, a need expressed in the Army recruitment slogan, "be all that you can be."

Following Maslow's theory, you would expect people naturally to look for the fulfillment of basic necessities first, personal pleasure second, and then to feel free to investigate the possibilities of altruism and self-giving. As Maslow knew, people hunger for "the good, the beautiful, and the true" just as they do for food. They prefer to live in a world at peace than a world at war, in a world of plenty rather than a world of famine, in a beautiful and healthy world rather than an ugly and polluted one. Given a choice, they prefer the positive to the negative.

## QUESTIONS OF VALUE

Your values are what give meaning to your live. Just as first level satisfaction is important because it addresses your financial requirements, and the second level because it addresses your personality and skills, this third level is crucial to a full enjoyment of your life and work because it is the place where your deepest values express themselves.

Steve Jobs, cofounder of the Apple computer company, lured John Sculley away from PepsiCo to become C.E.O. of Apple by asking him, "You don't want to spend the rest of your days selling sugared water to kids, do you?" According to Milton Moskowitz, coauthor of *The 100 Best Companies to Work for in America,* Sculley has since been heard to say, "At Apple we have a chance to change society."

What do you see as the purpose of life? What gives your life a sense of meaning? These are the kinds of standards against which real satisfaction in life is measured, and they are at the heart of real work satisfaction. Maybe you're not comfortable with that phrase, "the purpose of life." But what does your life strive toward? What are your deepest values? What is it that makes the all-important difference?

A sense of mission can express itself in a wide variety of ways. You may feel the need to run your own business, for example, or to influence the way things are done, or simply to be aware of the beauty all around you. Consider the German poet Rilke's description of the human mission:

> Yes, the springtimes needed you. Many stars
> waited for you to notice them. A wave
> rolled toward you out of the past, or, as you
> walked under an open window, a violin
> uttered itself. All this was your mission.
> But could you accomplish it?

Is life richest when you create or when you appreciate beauty? When you utilize your talents to the fullest? When you help others? In the final analysis, it is usually in terms of these bedrock values that we assess our lives. Yet these values can very easily get shoved aside by the pressures of everyday living. You may even feel that they are irrelevant to the task of getting a job, getting ahead, and putting yourself on a firm financial basis.

Particularly in the early stages of your working life, you may feel the need to downplay these values. The search for early financial success may make it seem advisable to overlook them. But by the time middle age and its attendant crises swing onto the horizon, most people are acclimatized to their financial situation, and have passed the initial burst of enthusiastic learning in their chosen profession. Then, often when it feels too late, many people realize that their job lacks fulfilment at the second and third levels, and that leaves them feeling very hollow in their forties and fifties.

These may not be values that you tend to examine every day, but they are vitally important. Your immediate satisfaction probably doesn't depend on them, but your long-range satisfaction may.

Choose one of the sentences below for completion, and write on it until you feel you have said enough to move on to another sentence. Work with the sentences that strike the most responsive chord in you. These sentence completions will allow you to put your deepest and most cherished values into words, perhaps for the first time. They will help you to remember just how important your values are, and how much satisfaction they could bring to your daily work.

— What's really most important to me is . . .

— To me, "making a contribution" means . . .

— I have a deep wish to understand . . .

— The area that I feel most passionately about is . . .

— In my life, I really value the search for . . .

— The quality that I admire above all in other people is . . .

— I have a real sense of commitment to . . .

— One value I'd like to see more of in my own life is . . .

— One of my deeply held values that my work allows me to express is . . .

— I'd feel most deeply satisfied if my work allowed me to . . .

Now sit back, relax, and imagine yourself doing work that embodies the values you have been considering. Don't let yourself be distracted by doubts or other considerations. Take your time, and savor the feeling of that kind of work. Imagine the sense of purpose your life would have.

Imagining work that embodies your deepest values will strengthen your sense of commitment and purpose. If you use the visualization technique discussed in Chapter Two, it may even provide you with clues as to how to go about finding that work. What might it look like, if you were making a transition from work that was satisfying at the first and second levels, to work that satisfied you on all three?

Let's take an example. Barry works for a bank. He spends his day in arbitrage in the money market. He would as happily sell as buy, and not surprisingly, a percentage rubs off on him. Barry really enjoys his work. He starts his day at 5 A.M., and stops at 2:30 P.M., because the markets on the East Coast have closed.

For Barry, the shift to satisfaction plus came when he decided to apply his enjoyment of the market to the needs of clients whose social purposes he liked. Many charities need someone to do the kind of work that Barry does expertly: investment counseling and brokerage.

Barry chose to spend at least part of each week consulting for charities like Save the Children, doing the work he enjoys for a cause he believes in. Now, when he makes a few thousand dollars, the children benefit too.

## BEING OF BENEFIT AND EXPRESSING VALUES

In choosing work, you may want to consider (1) the benefit that your work will bring to the world around you, and (2) the degree to which it will permit you to express your deepest and most profound values. This chapter is organized around these two approaches. The distinction between these two perspectives is important, because it offers you a choice of strategies.

The first approach, that of making a contribution, is the one taken by many of those who work in areas such as health care and education. It is an approach that affirms that the world needs the contribution you have to offer every bit as much as you wish to give it. This kind of approach doesn't necessarily involve the use of all your skills, nor can it always deliver much in the way of pay and office amenities. Working on a mailing for C.A.R.E. may not challenge your highest skills and talents, but the satisfaction it brings is that of seeing a real problem addressed.

The second approach is that of inspiration and creativity. A bassoonist, for example, is unlikely to have looked at the world and decided it lacked sufficient bassoon music. He or she is more likely to have discovered their own intense passion for music. Their gift is in expressing the music they find within themselves.

## SOMETHING MUST BE DONE

More and more people are coming to the conclusion that "something must be done about it." Just exactly what "it" is, of course, is an open question to which everyone has different answers. "It" may be the state of education, the type of medical care currently available, or the whole issue of nuclear weapons and world peace.

It is not the purpose of this book to provide political, moral, social, ethical, or ecological views. It is our purpose, however, to consider some of the issues that come up as we consider the "state of the planet," and to suggest ways in which your feelings about them can be related to your work.

This is another opportunity for you to take a look at the kinds of work you might wish to choose or avoid in making your contribution. Let's focus on some specific concerns that you may want to "do something about."

• Care of the Planet:

From air pollution to soil erosion, from off-shore oil drilling to the protection of whales, the care of the planet is a subject of growing concern.

Many of these ecological issues have a profound impact on questions of energy use, and the trade-offs are seldom simple. The same pipeline that threatens an ecosystem may prevent the need for a nuclear power plant. The nuclear power plant, in turn, raises questions of plant safety, nuclear waste disposal, and the transport of radioactive materials. And when these issues are raised, questions of nuclear weaponry and international terrorism are not far behind.

Where do you stand on the subject of agriculture? Do you feel that agribusiness is destroying small farms, and with it a knowledge of the land and its potential that has been passed down for centuries? Do you feel, perhaps, that the important thing is to increase the yield of crops by means of scientific research, and then to undertake massive land-reclamation projects in the Sahara?

Is technological medicine the wave of the future? Or does medicine need to return to the practices of an earlier age, to a recognition of the the healing power of suggestion, now known to medical science as the placebo effect?

Human rights is an umbrella phrase for another large area of concern. Do you have strong feelings about home care for the dying, child-abuse prevention, civil rights, and the plight of refugees? What about the homeless? Women's rights? The victims of violent crime?

Depending on the extent to which you feel that any one of these issues is a major concern of yours, you may decide to do a number of things. You might send a check to an organization that represents your view, volunteer some of your time, choose not to work in an industry that you feel is at odds with your own attitude, or actively seek full-time employment in an area that relates to one of these concerns.

• Daily Issues:

The issues that concern you may be closer to home than the ones discussed so far. You may feel uncomfortable about the business practices of the company you work for, or about the way they treat employees, their record on employee safety, or the quality of their product.

Are there social implications in the job you now hold that

don't sit comfortably with you? If so, the editors of *New Age Journal,* in their book, *Chop Wood, Carry Water,* describe one possible way out. A group of highly trained technicians came to feel that their values and their work were incompatible, but were reluctant to leave their jobs because they all had families to support. They teamed up and formed a group support network. Then, one at a time, each member of the group left his job. The other members supported them and their families until they found new work more suited to their values.

• Your Style of Contribution:

If you feel these issues relate to the kind of contribution you would like to make, there are some further questions you may want to think about. Do you want your contribution to be made in the area where you already have skills and work experience? Perhaps you'd do well to continue working at your present job and work "on the side" on an issue that concerns you, maybe volunteering your time. Or is there an issue that seems so pressing that you'd like to find a paid position in the field, even if it means working in a small office at a near-volunteer wage?

The different ways in which you might go about incorporating your values into your work situation need to be specifically tailored to your individual circumstances. Part Two of this book will investigate some possibilities. But in every case, the first step is to get a sense of the values you hold, and the importance they have in your life.

## THE INSPIRATIONAL APPROACH

The second approach to giving of oneself is more elusive. Where the first approach involves finding ways in which your work can contribute to the betterment of the world around you, the second approach is a matter of diving into your personal resources, and giving of your own humanity. This is the traditional approach of those who have "vocations in life," notably artists, spiritual leaders, healers, and educators.

Each of these vocations originally involved a feeling that one was "called." But there's no reason why people in these categories should enjoy a monopoly of inspired work.

Just what does inspiration mean? Certainly, it doesn't just mean the enthusiasm you feel from having come fresh out of a weekly motivational sales meeting or a quarterly management conference. It means, quite specifically, a tapping of deep inner resources.

The inspirational approach is not necessarily a matter of doing something that you wouldn't already do for the other levels of satisfaction. It's a matter of getting so caught up in it, so swept away, that what was already a pleasure becomes an art.

If you are to express your inner resources in such a way as to share the essence of your humanity with others, it will require you to work at a level of concentration that draws upon intuition, creativity, and self-giving. Those people who adopt the internal or inspirational approach to giving will become more involved in exploring their individual human natures, their deeper needs and satisfactions. They may find themselves resurrecting values and attitudes that they forgot they had.

They may also find themselves revitalizing specific jobs and vocations. These "resurrected" vocations are important precisely because the values they embody tend to be overlooked or undervalued in this technology-oriented culture.

The traditional vocations brought great satisfaction to many of those who practiced them. This is no longer the case. Doctors have among the highest suicide rates of any profession. Teachers are increasingly susceptible to job burnout. Indeed, there are now several books which are specifically designed to help teachers get out of teaching and find other work. And recent studies show that blue-collar and clerical workers suffer from stress as much as do executives.

What happened? Why are some professions now so obviously less satisfying? And why do workers in general seem less satisfied today?

Many vocations seem to be suffering from "slippage," a kind of slow erosion of human values. The discontent that Studs Terkel noticed in so many workers indicates that it has taken root across the board in the world of work.

A number of doctors we know have gone through intense self-questioning about their profession. Jim was doing a brisk business in state-of-the-art neurosurgery for patients with serious back problems. But many of his patients were returning, often in less than two years. Despite having gone through a lot of pain, surgery, and expense, they were unimproved.

It can be extremely depressing to observe the continued suffering of one's patients and to be conscious of one's own evident ineffectiveness. Jim stopped operating, left his partnership, and spent a year studying pain. He researched techniques for pain management with physicians across the United States and in Europe. He brought back the best of these techniques and developed a "back clinic" for people with severe, chronic pain. He still performs occasional surgery when it is appropriate. But largely he uses exercise, diet, pain management, and counseling; drugs and surgery are very sparingly applied.

Jim has certainly not "gone native" and thrown out the high technology of modern science: but in some ways he has returned to an earlier and more traditional form of healing. His current practice is less invasive, and emphasizes the patient's innate capacity to heal.

If you feel that you have a sense of vocation about work you do, but that somehow the satisfaction you expected from your contribution isn't there anymore, you might want to check whether there has been "vocational slippage." Before you decide to give up on your current work, ask yourself whether it's your vocation that you need to rejuvenate, or whether it's genuinely the work that no longer satisfies.

The problem of "slipped" vocations frequently boils down to the fact that they have lost all trace of the third satisfaction, the satisfaction of serving, of going beyond oneself. In some cases, only the first level of satisfaction remains.

## FINDING YOUR ARCHETYPAL VOCATION

Perhaps you are not the kind of person who has a burning desire to go out there and change the world, nor do you find any evidence of "inspired resources" that you wish to contribute. Plenty of people feel there is no work that really calls to them.

It may well be that the reason this third-level stuff hasn't worked for you so far is because you haven't yet found the right context. Employment positions alter with each change in a civilization, a culture, a technology. The predispositions, talents and interests hardwired into people from birth are in some cases very ancient, while in others they are utterly new, addressed to a future whose needs cannot be rationally foreseen. It may be that the kind of work for which you are best suited does not exist as a job description currently in use in our society.

The psychologist Carl Jung observed that his patients' dreams were often filled with symbols from ancient myths and legends. He suggested that at a deep, unconscious level, we tend to come to grips with the fortunes and misfortunes of our lives in terms of these mythic patterns, which he referred to as "archetypes." Jung believed that these archetypes exert a powerful fascination in people's lives. He noted that "the greatest and best thoughts of man shape themselves upon these primordial images as upon a blueprint." They are, he argued, the source of meaning in our lives.

One of the major characters in *Walking on Air,* an enchanting novel by Pierre Delattre, is a circus high-wire performer called the Great Mamouli. Towards the end of the book, she discusses the place of archetypal and mythic roles in life and work:

> I have never believed that the ordinary black and white newspaper reality is worth living—the world according to *Time* magazine and television. I've been inspired to perform impossible feats ever since childhood when my mother read me fairy tales. I believe . . . that we can truly be happy only when we put on our legendary masks and take on our mythic roles . . . Whether we're to become high priestess, hermit, fool, sorcerer, merchant prince, magician, clown, warrior king, or lady in heaven, we can't be satisfied until we join ourselves to a great tradition.

If these words stir something within you, if myths and fairytales move you, if you prefer Tolkien to TV, you might consider the possibility of thinking about your work in terms of mythology. This doesn't necessarily mean that you find a specific archetype and then translate it into a job description. It simply means that you allow yourself to sense an archetypal dimension in your work.

Where does one look to find archetypal role models, or to nourish one's sense of meaning in this way?

— You can read mythology, and look for role models among the figures represented in Greek, Norse, or Native American myths.

— You can look back over history, and find your models in jobs that existed in former times.

— You can read science fiction, and discover future archetypes.

— Or you can research anthropology, and look to other cultures for your models.

Some people may find they are already living out a mythic role, without having made any deliberate choice to do so. Ralph

Nader, a champion of the individual consumer versus the large corporation, can be seen as a David taking on Goliath.

Some people discover an archetype that means so much to them that they find a way to translate it into an actual job. What, for instance, might you do if you identify with Scheherezade, the storyteller in *A Thousand and One Nights*? Tom Doty is someone who felt drawn to the ancient vocation of storytelling, and now earns his living at it. He draws his inspiration and material from the great storytellers and rich lore of the Kwakiutl, Tlingit, and other native peoples of the Pacific Northwest. Doty presents his stories around campfires, in hospitals, and at universities. In choosing to live out a mythic role, he has found a contemporary way to share some ancient insights.

Others find that a specific archetype deepens their sense of the work they already do. A Chinese Feng Shui master is a professional who is part architect and interior decorator, part meteorologist and ecologist, and part psychologist and shaman. An architect or interior designer might read Sarah Rossbach's book, *Feng Shui—the Chinese Art of Placement,* and obtain a whole new perspective on their profession.

Some may sense that they are suited to play some archetypal role, but need to adapt it to the realities of the twentieth-century workplace. During the Middle Ages, a court jester was someone who made the court a healthier place by poking fun at the king in precisely those areas where he was getting a bit above himself. A jester had to have a real flair for the job, since mocking kings could land one on the chopping block. One of the jester's skills was the ability to talk to the king with humor, and without fear.

What if you decide that the archetype of the court jester, say, fits your personality? Obviously, outside of Shakespeare festivals, there are few openings for court jesters. The first thing you must do is to recognize and accept what manner of person you are. Then you can explore ways of easing into the marketplace so that you perform your role and still manage to draw a regular paycheck.

If you fit a court jester archetype, there may be work for you in management consulting. Your work will then be "under-cover" in the sense that we discuss in Chapter Nine. It will involve improving the social dynamics of the workplaces where you consult as well as introducing new management skills and techniques.

D. Verne Morland, who works in management training and information management for NCR, wrote an article in *New Management* which suggests a need for court jesters in the modern business environment. His article included a detailed job description for a "Corporate Fool, Renaissance Wit," who would report to the Chief Executive Officer. "Since the ability to think creatively about the future is inversely proportional to the weight of today's responsibilities," it reads in part, "the fool should feel obligated only to: stir up controversy, respect no authority, and resist pressures to engage in detailed analyses.

"The incumbent must avoid verbs like study, analyze, plan, develop, refine, and assure in favor of verbs like associate, explore, synthesize, and stimulate. He (or she) should neither lead nor follow, but should stand outside the normal chain of command.

"The fool must exploit his intellectual carte blanche. She must ask outrageous questions and challenge basic assumptions. He must seek accuracy, not precision; originality, not consistency; insight, not completeness." And so on.

More generally, you might consider viewing the entire business world in an archetypal light. Beverly Potter's recent book, *The Way of the Ronin: A Guide to Career Strategy*, offers an unorthodox approach to career planning based on the legendary freelance samurai warriors or ronin of Japan. Part of the interest of her book lies in the fact that she not only recommends that individual entrepreneurs see themselves as contemporary ronin, she also suggests that these are "ronin times," not unlike those that prevailed at the end of the Tokugawa dictatorship in Japan.

Dr. Potter is not the first writer to explore ronin strategies in the context of the contemporary business world. In 1645 Miyamoto Musashi wrote *Book of Five Rings,* a book of samurai strategy. Three hundred and thirty-five years later it became a best-seller in America as a textbook for businessmen which presented the Japanese "code of Bushido" under the subtitle, "The Real Art of Japanese Management."

Management consultant Roger Harrison, in a recent article in *Human Resources Management,* suggests that "there is some-thing of the hero in all of us," and that the business leader of the future "shares the characteristics which Joseph Campbell discusses in *The Hero with a Thousand Faces,"* one of the best modern introductions to mythological thinking. Harrison goes on to describe the new leader as "a secure and mature individual who can articulate values and high principles that give organiza-tional life meaning, but who is more receptive and self-aware than we normally expect . . . leaders to be."

## THE ULTIMATE SIGN-UP SHEET

If Utopia, the Kingdom, a month of Sundays, Paradise, or whatever else you might care to call it were to be established on earth, and you were to be a subcontractor, which part would you want to be involved in? Which part of rewriting the script of the world would you personally be interested in? What is your myth? Where do your values lie?

To bring these issues to a close, try the following sentence completions:

— What I love best about this world of ours, and would really enjoy contributing to, is . . .

— The area of work that really inspires me, and through which I can pass on the fruits of that inspiration to others, is . . .

— The project I'd most like to see get under way is . . .

— I'd be honored to be involved in . . .

— I'd love to be part of an international team working to . . .

— I'm beginning to realize that my work will mean most to me when it . . .

Imagine the world that you'd like to see, with yourself and your work a part of it.

# ZENNING IT

**Relevance:** For those who find their present work less than satisfying—and feel stuck with it, at least for now.

**Premise:** The way to make even a boring job fulfilling is to get the most out of yourself.

**Strategy:** By changing your attitude you can change the quality of attention, and so increase the satisfaction you feel at even a humdrum task.

**Tactics:** Exploring the zen-like quality of "present focus"; using creativity on the job; creating a game; finding art in your work; using your work as a teacher; finding rhythm in your work; Inner Game techniques; winning when you lose; and excellence.

# Chapter 6

## ZENNING IT

*There are certain natures to whom the work is nothing, the act of working, everything.*

Arthur Symonds

The single, simplest way to enjoy your work is to enjoy it. This may sound like circular reasoning, and if you don't enjoy your work right now it may even read like a Catch-22. Let's just say that, infuriating as it may seem, it contains an important clue to work satisfaction.

If you feel dissatisfied with your work, you can start changing things in one of two places. You can either look for ways to change the work, or you can change yourself. Whichever place you start, the impact from one will certainly spill over into the other.

The strategies in this chapter are partly designed to help those who feel unable to get out of their present work situation: they are strategies for "making the most of a bad job." But you'll find they can help you make the most of a good job, too.

Every instinct in us rebels at the thought of giving ourselves fully to work that we would never choose if financial and other considerations didn't dictate it to us. Yet it is our attitude toward work, rather than the work itself, that sets the tone for the way in which forty hours of our week will be spent. Attitude can make, in Milton's words, "a Heav'n of Hell, a Hell of Heav'n."

What Milton observed three hundred years ago is still the case. "New attitudes change the very experience of daily work," author Marilyn Ferguson notes in *The Aquarian Conspiracy.* "Work becomes a ritual, a game, a discipline, an adventure, learning, even an art, as our perceptions change. The stress of tedium and the stress of the unknown, the two causes of work-related suffering, are transformed. A more fluent quality of attention allows us to move through tasks that once seemed repetitious or distasteful. . . . We see that meaning can be discovered and expressed in any human service: cleaning, teaching, gardening, carpentry, selling, caring for children, driving a taxi." New attitudes which will result in a more fluent quality of attention are what this chapter is all about.

## TECHNIQUES FOR HANDLING BOREDOM AND OVERLOAD

Marilyn Ferguson touched on the two main reasons why people don't involve themselves in their work: because it is too boring or too demanding. Dissimilar as they are, these conditions both lead to frustration and stress, and block the interest and enthusiasm that bring work satisfaction.

Boredom is the sense that only a small part of one's potential is being used. This does not apply only to people whose work is repetitive and dull. Airline pilots can get pretty bored when the plane is on automatic pilot, just as a billing clerk can get bored entering invoices into a computerized accounting system eight hours a day. That's why choosing work that uses as much of your skills and interests as possible is so important. But many people just don't work at fascinating, challenging jobs.

At the opposite end of the scale are the people who feel too much challenge. If boredom means that you are "only firing on two cylinders," then "overload" is what happens when too much is demanded of you. It's possible to feel as overloaded when you're expected to answer five incoming calls while you're also receiving clients in the executive reception area, as it is to run a multi-million dollar company. The details may be different, but overload is overload, whatever your work.

No one can tell you how to make a boring job utterly exciting, or an impossible task possible. There are, however, techniques which can bring creativity and enthusiasm back into your job so that the boring will become more interesting or the impossible more possible.

Not all of these techniques will work in all circumstances. The technique that works today may not work tomorrow. The aim here is to provide you with a wide range of options.

## WHY "ZENNING IT"?

There's a particular attitude that sums up everything this chapter suggests—the attitude with which a zen student goes about the day's work. "Zenning it" is the answer to both boredom and overload.

The little word "zen" can stand for many things. It is the name of a school of Japanese Buddhism which emphasizes the practice of meditation. It refers to the distinctive style that this tradition has contributed to world culture. It is a style of art, of poetry, every line clean and spare. Above all, it means a certain down-to-earth, no-nonsense spirit that the old zen masters embodied, and which zen students today still work to attain.

Zen, as the term is used here, has nothing directly to do with Buddhism or anything oriental. Here, zen is simply a metaphor. Think of it as zen with a small "z". "Zenning it" is a phrase which indicates a certain quality of attention to what one is doing.

This zen spirit has a great deal to do with work, and the way one goes about it. Indeed, one celebrated maxim speaks of zen as basically a matter of "chopping wood and carrying water":

getting on with the work of one's life without distraction or fuss. When a doctor approached the zen master Nan-in and asked to be taught zen, Nan-in replied "Treat your patients kindly." When the doctor protested that he wanted to learn more, Nan-in told him "A physician shouldn't waste his time here. Get back to your patients."

Let's take a look at the way "zenning it" can operate in the mailroom of a New York advertising firm.

Ernie was master of his mailroom, back in the fifties. He'd never even heard of zen. But wrap a package? You couldn't wrap a package better than Ernie could. There wasn't an inch of string thrown away. He had wrapping down to a science. He also had it down to an art.

Dispatch it to 222 West 23rd Street? Ernie would tell you, "Sure, between 7th and 8th. Tony's the doorman." He knew the map. He knew the city streets. He knew the subway system. In his own way, Ernie had the mastery of New York City. Needless to say, Ernie was able to get the job done in about half the time anyone else could.

That kind of excellence is what this chapter is about.

"Zenning it" is at the heart of all success. It makes running a mailroom, or doing any other kind of work, an entirely different experience. It is present in a child's absorption with a new toy, in the attention you pay when you're watching a gripping movie, in the commitment of the successful salesman, in the artist's dedication to his or her work. And it is specifically trained into the zen monk as the core secret of existence.

It is very simple.

It's a trick, an open secret. It's a matter of being present at your own life, not just showing up for the roll call. And the only way to manage that is to stay in "present focus."

● Present Focus:

Staying in present focus is the master technique of this chapter. As long as you're absorbed in what you're doing, no matter what it is, you won't be thinking about the end of the day and watching the minutes tick by. It's a straightforward strategy, but one to which few people give much thought.

When you show up for a task, really show up. Be there. Pay close attention to what you are doing. Focus on it. And do it. Fully. In the words of another zen saying, "When you stand, stand. When you walk, walk. Don't wobble."

Simple, zen masters call it, and it is. In fact it's so simple, it's virtually impossible. No matter how hard you try to focus on what you're doing, you get distracted by irrelevant thoughts and worries. Your mind wanders off on ten thousand different tangents. That "simple" focus is lost.

This problem of the mind wandering, and the need to bring it back, crops up all the time in zen meditation. You might almost say that if the mind didn't wander, zen would be out of business.

Here's the procedure. Whenever you catch your mind wandering, the first thing is to notice where it went, and why. Very quickly. Make a note of any business that needs to be attended to. Put your concerns on hold. Then bring your attention back to the task, and continue with it. The idea is to stay in the present, to become completely absorbed.

- Ritual:

One way to begin the workday in present focus is to devise a small ritual. Television's locker-room coverage has made everyone familiar with the pregame rituals of professional athletes. These rituals are intended to lift the players into "the right spirit" for peak performance—and you can apply the same strategy to the beginning of your workday.

Many people find that a "clearing ritual," in which they set out their equipment or clear their desks and arrange their papers, does a great deal to set them up for a successful day at work. It moves them from the hurried and harried state that driving through the morning traffic can cause, into a calmer and more focused attitude as they prepare for work.

Jobs frequently involve a series of "opening moves" that one must do each day. Cashiers and bank tellers have to count and verify the cash in their drawers before they start the day's business. Many people finalize the day's schedule as they drink their first cup of coffee. Others have a ten-minute update with the members of their team.

Rather than treat these inevitable setting-up routines as tedious chores, you may want to formalize them slightly, so as to take advantage of their potential as focusing and centering rituals. The repetition of an accustomed task and the act of tidying away everything not directly relevant to the business at hand, combine to create a mood of readiness and alert attention. A similar "clearing" at the end of the day can help you wind down from the day's work, and leave the office without "carrying away a briefcaseful in your head."

Now let's consider a variety of other techniques for bringing the zen spirit into the workplace.

• Riding the Waves:

There are always situations you'd prefer were some way other than the way they are. Like waves, they can capsize you, or you can ride them. The real art is to maintain a balance between concern and the lack of it.

First, you care. You care about your work. You give it your best shot. And when you've taken care, you worry as little as possible: you become carefree. If things don't work out in the way you intended, there's very little to be gained by letting them gnaw at you. You can't do better than your best.

It's not just a matter of dropping the whole issue and not coming back to it, though. The results come in. Maybe the contract was awarded to another supplier. Perhaps your inventory control program still has bugs, or the advertising campaign you designed just isn't delivering the sales. You try to analyze the failure. You go back to the beginning. You start over. And you care.

Do just this, again and again, and many of the difficulties of the workplace will disappear.

- A Personalized Approach:

People tend to think the old saw, "All work and no play makes Jack a dull boy," means that Jack should quit his workaholic ways and take his family for a vacation now and again. They seldom think of bringing a sense of play into the workplace. Yet that's what on-the-job creativity boils down to; and it's the most direct route to making your job less boring and more fulfilling.

Suppose your work isn't going too well. Try to stop seeing that as a problem, in the sense of a difficulty, and begin to look at it as a problem in the sense of an opportunity or challenge.

Perhaps you're bored, and have turned yourself off at some deep level of your being. You are no longer in present focus, you're on automatic pilot. You need to deliberately turn yourself back on again and "be present" at the job. Your problem is to find ways to make your job less routine and more demanding, which means you need to make some special demands on yourself.

The suggestions in the rest of this chapter will give you a range of possible ways to "be present." But your own creativity will be needed to supply the specifics. You need to take a personalized approach.

Maybe you're overloaded. Perhaps you're gritting your teeth, trying hard to stay on top of things, and maybe busting your guts and/or your marriage in the process. Sometimes people try and try, and try too hard. In effect, you may be trying to cure your overload by overloading yourself even more. On the other hand, you may sigh, roll your eyes questioningly, and let the work quietly go to hell.

Again, your problem is to relax enough to bring your enthusiasm and self-confidence back into the picture. Simply getting away from the overwhelmed feeling and into a confident, alert state will make the task seem less formidable. Sort through the techniques in this chapter, find the ones you're going to try, and then apply your creativity to tailor them to your circumstances. In other words, take a personalized approach.

- Making a Game of It:

One useful strategy is to turn your work into play by creating a game that you can play while you're doing your job.

Let's say you're a medical technician who checks blood samples for everything from cholesterol to leukemia. You have a microscope, and some of the most fascinating things the human eye has ever seen come under your gaze every day. When the pressure gets to you, take a minute—that's all you need—and imagine for a moment you're an art critic, and the specimens on your slide are pictures.

How do you feel about what you see? How are the colors? Does this slide look better when you make it slightly out of focus? That's Impressionism. Do the crystalline structures remind you of Mondrian? Paul Klee? Kandinsky? Your minute's up. But your mood has changed, and you're more relaxed.

A harassed bartender turned one of the most frustrating aspects of his work into a game. Some of the customers at his bar were what he called "bromides," people whose conversation is so boring it puts other people to sleep. Unfortunately, as the bartender, he couldn't afford to doze off every time one of them came into his bar. But he could and did become a connoisseur of bores.

He started to note the clichés of his trade; the phrases he heard time and again that would have had him yawning if he hadn't been so busy.

"Let's see, I'll have a gin and tonic, a vodka tonic, a whiskey sour, and two white wines. They're not all for me, by the way."

"I don't know how you bartenders remember all those drinks. I have trouble remembering what day it is."

"What's good for a cold?"

"One more like that and you'll have to carry me out of here."

Our friend jotted them all down on cocktail napkins, and although he spent a year gathering his definitive collection, he swears you can hear most of them in a single night.

The lab technician and the bartender each devised a game that increased their enjoyment while giving them something of a break from the stresses of their work.

Create a game for yourself.

Terry is a bagger in a grocery store. When he packs a customer's groceries into the sack, he tries to pack the items in such a way that they come out "level" at the fill-line. He's playing a work game.

Suppose you're a short-order cook on the lunch shift. Pretty soon, you begin to recognize the faces of the regulars. Being people of regular habits, they probably order the same thing most days. You can soon look at a face sitting down at the counter, and remember, "Here comes tuna salad on rye, hold the onion." Take it a stage further. Listen to their tone of voice when they order and decide what kind of a mood they are in. Write a novel or a soap opera in your head in which your regulars play their parts day by day.

You are playing a work game.

• See Your Work as an Art Form:

At Benihana's, a chain of Japanese restaurants, the chefs have turned the cutting of food into an art form. They twirl their knives through the air and catch them. They slice your shrimp to look like butterflies. When they are cooking the shrimps and vegetables, they toss them elegantly into the air. The Benihana chefs' style is an expression of Japan's long tradition of aesthetics, which derives in turn from that same zen spirit. When you find the art in your work, real mastery comes.

What can be done in other jobs to express an aesthetic sense? The record store clerk who arranges the display of featured performers and groups can do more than just line the records up. He or she can sequence the pictures and colors of the record jackets to create an attractive arrangement. The care and skill with which a waiter folds napkins and sets the table makes a difference. The personal assistant who does a really good job of visual layout on the presentation he types up gets satisfaction from knowing that presentation reads well, but he also receives an aesthetic pleasure from his work.

Every action can be performed with a sense of aesthetics. Japanese culture understands this very well: in the tea ceremony, a flower arrangement, or the design of an entire garden, nothing is unconsidered. But the occasion needn't be special or significant. Even the most mundane task in the simplest setting can become an expression of art; even the simplest gesture can be a dance.

• See Your Work as a Teacher:

People work best when they are learning. In fact, boredom could probably be described quite simply as the feeling you get when there's too little to learn. The strategy here is to take the situation in which you find yourself as a given, and treat it as a teacher. Your first move might be to let the events of the day suggest the lessons you should learn. What exactly was the point at which you became bored? How come you did the same task yesterday without switching off? Is there something else irritating you?

If your task is repetitive, what are the things that slow you down? How much does your mood have to do with how well you perform? What happens when you're angry? Tired? Depressed? Fresh in from the weekend? Exhausted after the weekend? You may have ready answers to all these questions, but set them aside for now. Watch yourself while you work, and discover the difference between the boring times and the times when you're right there, so you can renew your confidence in your ability to avoid boredom.

It doesn't really matter what you learn. If you're learning, you won't be bored. And since human beings find themselves and their own inner workings an endlessly fascinating study, that's as good a place as any to start.

You can also look at your situation and decide on an aspect of your work to investigate. Scott worked at a hamburger stand while he was in high school, and turned the job into a classroom. He wanted to find out what other people were all about, so he turned his cashier's job into an experiment in human relations. "It was the first time I'd ever had to talk with strangers," he said, "and I wanted to learn how you do that. My manager wanted me to sell side orders, and I wanted to get to know people, so one of my first tasks was to discover how you ask a customer, 'Would you like some potato cakes, too?' or 'Will that be a large coke?' in such a way that they feel like saying 'Yes.' The manager got the increased sales she was looking for, and I discovered a new confidence that was pretty wonderful for someone just shedding a 15-year-old's awkwardness."

Scott needed to learn about restaurant management and advertising as part of a work-study program at school. He asked his manager to introduce him to the franchise owner, and the franchise owner ("the first millionaire I ever met") showed him how to analyze the sales impact of a seven-inch newspaper coupon, and talked to him about advertising layout and design. Scott learned from his customers. He learned from his boss. He learned from the people who delivered the produce. For Scott, there was always something to learn.

Discovering what there is to learn requires creativity. What can you learn in the course of your everyday work? How much can you learn about the equipment you use? What can you learn about your fellow workers or clients? About the businesses that interact with yours? Can you learn how to run two tasks together, to streamline work?

You might want to learn how to express problems to your

boss in such a way that they get heard. Notice how you feel when you come into the room to talk to the boss. Does your enthusiasm for your ideas get the better of you? Or are you so timid, that you're almost out of the room before you've made your first point?

What time of day is it best to approach the boss? Does it help to have a written presentation that covers the facts, and then let yourself get the message across in a few broad strokes? Can you tie your points in with any of his or her pet projects or peeves?

Whatever your situation, you can always use it as an opportunity to learn something new. Creativity can show you endless possibilities.

Specifically, you can learn about what can be done to improve the way your job is conducted. What can you learn that would most directly improve your circumstances at work?

As an insurance underwriter, Phil often found himself asking the same follow-up questions over the phone day after day. So he set himself the task of increasing the efficiency of the forms the agents sent him. Were there any extra questions that the agents could ask their clients that would save a lot of telephone time later on? How could the forms best be redesigned?

If your job has problems, study them. What can be done to "cure" the job? To streamline it? To humanize it? Bring your present focus to bear not only on the work you do, but on the results you achieve. Learn from the feedback this alertness brings you. Where are the bottlenecks in procedure? By keeping an open mind and paying close attention to the flow and rhythm of your work, you may be able to learn your way into a more interesting, and less frustrating, situation.

- Find a Rhythm to Your Work:

For many who don't enjoy their work, routine is perhaps the worst part of it. One of the simplest routes to satisfaction in any task is to find its natural rhythm. Rhythm is the opposite of routine.

Consider the various rhythms that already rule our lives. Day and night, waking and sleeping. In-breath and out. Some rhythms are seasonal: spring and fall. Some are lifelong: youth and old age, birth and death. Others are rhythms that are found in all human activity. Tension and relaxation. Effort and break-through. Work and play.

Rhythms such as these are natural to all living creatures, and if you can find natural rhythms of this sort in your work, recognize and enjoy them, you are more likely to feel good about your work as a whole. It may seem almost too obvious for words, and yet it's easy to forget: work that "never lets up" is almost always less satisfying than the kind that has periodic rhythms built into it.

Jonathan is a successful wine salesman who works for one of the big California distributors. Like most outside salesmen, his work involves a rhythm composed of merchandising and travel. When Jonathan has to travel a long distance to make one important sale, he begins to find driving all those damn freeways very frustrating. However, when he makes a large number of local sales, he sometimes wishes he could get into the car, and be alone with his radio and the freeway for a while.

Jonathan's perfect day has a rhythm to it, a rhythm of talking with restaurant owners, informing, persuading, selling, and then travel, solitude, time for reflection. The important thing to note here is that while either of these components is enjoyable in moderation, both of them become fatiguing when they are not balanced by their opposite.

Not everyone can find work that incorporates such clear-cut rhythms, of course—but anything that brings rhythm and patterned variation into your work will tend to refresh your attitude toward it. Even something as simple as taking your coffee breaks away from your desk will help.

— Notice the rhythms in your work.

— Notice how long you tend to be involved in one task as opposed to another. Notice when you get up and walk about.

— See if you can't make a balanced rhythm of these things.

The anthropologist Edward T. Hall found that American executives tend to schedule meetings back-to-back, while their European colleagues schedule fewer events in the same amount of time, and described themselves as feeling less pressed for time as a result.

Take time out from any continuous task and vary it with another task, so as to give yourself a chance to relax from that particular form of effort. Find a rhythm to your work, and dance to it.

● Unwinding:

Suppose that you're feeling bored or overloaded, and attempts to stay in present focus just aren't working. Is there anything you can do to directly release the frustration and stress?

When the pressure gets to you, you can sometimes benefit by "slipping your mind into something more comfortable." You can let your mind wander—not in the direction of self-doubt, or worry, or irritation, but in the direction of relaxation. You can unwind. Alternating spells of intense concentration and activity with brief periods of relaxation not only gives a rhythm to your day, it gives you a second wind when you most need it.

Dr. Herbert Benson in his book, *The Relaxation Response,* describes the simplest and most profound focusing technique of all. Here are the instructions:

1. Give your mind an internal focus of attention, such as your breathing. Simply pay attention to your point of focus. As

you breathe naturally in and out, be aware of your breath; be aware of any tension in your shoulders, and the gentle lifting of your breath. Allow your breathing to soothe and massage those tensions away. Be aware of the way your breathing gets deeper as you relax. Simply be aware of your breath.

2. Don't pay any attention to distracting thoughts. If you worry about the time, that's a distraction. If you'd like to kill your boss, that's a distraction (it would be homicide, too, but that's beside the point). If you wonder whether the technique is working, that's a distraction. When distracting thoughts come up, don't worry about them. Think of them as though they were passing clouds on a sunny day. Let them pass.

3. If your mind wanders from its focus, bring it back again. Let your thoughts evaporate, let them slip away, then quietly bring your attention back to the steady flow of your breathing.

Ideally, you should learn the relaxation response in a quiet environment where you won't be disturbed, sitting comfortably with your eyes closed. Once you have learned it, you can use it as a "one-minute" technique in the middle of a busy day at the office. When you've relaxed, you can bring your state of alert concentration back onto the job.

One last hint about unwinding: having a sense of humor helps. The slightly stale jokes you hear at the office may make you laugh a lot more there than they would at home, and there's a reason for it. Too many of us are "wound up like a spring" by the time we've been at work for a few hours. Looking for the humor in your situation, finding a chuckle, a quiet laugh, a guffaw, literally shakes down the tired muscles and changes the blood chemistry of the brain.

## THE INNER GAME

Let's take a look at some of the ways a master strategist has dealt with these same issues.

As befits someone who was captain of the Harvard tennis team, Timothy Gallwey is both a tennis pro and something of a philosopher. His first book, *The Inner Game of Tennis,* created such an impact that his methods were soon applied to the teaching not only of tennis, but of skiing, music, weight loss, sales, and computer skills.

Gallwey's secret is his understanding of the ways in which people learn best. He calls it the "Inner Game." Archie McGill, former head of AT&T's Advanced Information Systems, declared recently that in business, "the Inner Game is the game of the future."

AT&T phone operators experience both boredom and stress in the course of a day's work. Imagine spending your entire day fielding an average of 700 phone enquiries and complaints. No sooner is one call answered than another one comes up for you to handle, with an average of less than a one second gap between them. And many of those callers are either frustrated, impatient, or angry.

AT&T invited Tim Gallwey's Inner Game Corporation to examine ways to make the job less threatening and more interesting. Gallwey's solution was to offer the operators "a way to control their experience."

"We had them listen and try to imagine what each customer looked like, to use their faculties to make the experience more interesting," Gallwey said. One specific indicator that Gallwey asked the operators to listen for was a quality in the callers' voices: warmth or irritation, sexiness or vitality. Gallwey asked them to evaluate, moment by moment, the intensity of the voice quality on a scale of one to ten.

When the callers were frustrated and angry, the operators

might decide to keep up a running tally in their heads of just how angry the voices on the other end of the line sounded. "That's an eight . . . nine . . . eight . . . steady at eight," and so on. By practicing this simple awareness technique, the operators were able to accomplish a number of things:

1. They changed the game. They now had an additional task to perform, a task which did not relate directly to their official business of answering the callers' questions.

2. They could therefore feel involved in the calls in a way that effectively sidetracked their sense of being under attack. The callers' anger became something to be aware of, rather than something to be taken personally.

3. They were thus able to answer their callers' questions without their own frustrated response to frustration getting in the way of clear thinking.

4. As their own calmness began to filter through to their callers, the callers' own frustration level often decreased.

5. The operators were then able to get positive, immediate feedback on their one to ten scale as to the success of the new game plan.

6. Boredom was reduced by the addition of a "human interest" component in their work, and stress reduced through the use of this defusing technique.

7. As a result, the job became less pressured and monotonous, and more fascinating. And at the end of the day, the operators could feel the difference.

"It's terrific," a supervisor commented. "When you're relaxed, you move faster, you flow, you're not tensed up, you think properly." An operator added, "it helps you control yourself and be more of an observer. And it seems like the customers are different, because you handle them differently."

Gallwey's strategy is profoundly simple: change the game. Don't think about success and failure, just concentrate on the details of what you are doing. Concentrate on some aspect of the task that allows you to learn by getting feedback. Let pure awareness of what is going on lift you out of judgment and self-doubt.

- Winning When You Lose:

One other story about Tim Gallwey. He set out along the path that led him to the inner game theory, his string of best-sellers and his current work with AT&T and a variety of other giant corporations the day he lost match point in the National Boy's Championship. It was his first major tournament, and Gallwey was winning against a high-ranked opponent. He knew it. He had only one point to make to reach the quarter finals, and the pressure got to him. He served a double fault, missed an easy volley, and went on to lose game, set and match.

Out of that defeat, Gallwey built his success. He asked himself again and again why he had spoiled those critical shots. The answer he discovered was that he missed because of a "hidden" opponent in his head; a part of himself that was so keen to win, so scared of losing, that it froze up his usual level of ability.

Quite apart from the insights you can derive from the rest of Gallwey's approach, there's an insight in that story itself. Tim Gallwey's lost match point looked like defeat at the time, but he turned it into victory.

Hard times are painful. They may be flagrantly unfair. They may seem impossible to cope with. But the mistakes you make, even the times you may be fired, can be times of growth and discovery.

Thousands of people besides Tim Gallwey have built successes out of earlier failures. Learning to turn your losses into gains is a large part of work satisfaction.

## EXCELLENCE

Perhaps the single most interesting question you could ask about people and the work satisfaction they receive is this: What's the difference between the people who just pull through and the ones who wind up really successful at a job they love?

Let's take another look at Scott. We left him at the cash register of a hamburger stand in Lincoln, Nebraska, where he was learning to make friends (and influence people). Scott's now twenty-three and lives in Los Angeles. As well as developing some of his own projects, Scott puts in a nine-to-five day doing office management, and sometimes helping out with reception. Since we last saw him, he has also:

— stage-managed and done the lighting for a series of concert tours;

— created and developed a children's TV cartoon project; and

— been a national champion in the twenty-kilometer race-walk ten times.

We believe that Scott's a winner, and that the way he goes about his work has a great deal to do with his success. He feels that in order to do his office job to his own complete satisfaction he needs to be on top of all the details. And he brings to his job the kind of detailed attention he learned while working the 150 lighting cues in an average concert. He feels the work he does in the reception area demands an ability to be courteous and warm with clients, and his former training while selling hamburgers certainly helps. He realizes that he needs energy and enthusiasm, and considers the three fifteen-mile runs he takes every week an investment in his work, as well as an appropriate training for his Olympic goals.

And Scott's learning. He knows that the success of his cartoon project will depend partly on his ability to deal effectively with people in the entertainment industry, lawyers, agents, promoters and studio moguls, and he regards his office work as good training for the business world. "It's a great discipline for learning attention, patience, and courtesy," he says. He also uses the time when he's sticking 600 labels onto envelopes to devise new plots for his cartoon characters.

"My goal is to experience personal excellence," he told us, "because that's our potential. I'd like to achieve excellence as an athlete, and bring my body to the point of real artistry and mastery. And I'd like to do the same with my mind. Once you touch the edge of excellence, you never want to forget it."

You may well hear about Scott before too long—perhaps because he wins an Olympic medal, or because his cartoon series is the hottest thing this side of Sesame Street, or for any one of half a dozen other reasons. When you do, it will be because of his attitude: his willingness to change his work into a classroom; to transform a mid-level office job into a staging ground for his TV and film projects; and his intense willingness to explore and utilize every gift he has.

The key to extraordinary success is really quite simple. It can be learned at a hamburger stand, while answering phones, selling wholesale, or managing an office. It's the attitude of excellence, and there's no substitute for it.

● Just the Details:

This chapter has suggested a number of things you can do to enhance your interest in your work, or to distract you from it long enough to get a break and feel refreshed. But the goal is to get past the stage where you're patching up a not-so-satisfactory job, to the place where you achieve real excellence and the satisfaction that goes with it. That's what "present focus" allows you to do, and that's where the satisfaction of accomplishment comes in.

Doing a really fine job is also one of the surest ways to make more money. Do your job brilliantly, and if the person you're working for doesn't appreciate it, somebody else will.

A student who was remodeling the kitchen at her local zen center looked up as she was putting the finishing touches to her work, and saw the resident zen master had come into the room.

"How is it going?" he asked her.

"Everything's fine," she replied. "I've just got a few details to finish up."

The zen master looked puzzled. "But it's all a matter of details. Details are all there are," he said.

Pay attention. Create your ritual, and stick with it. Start your work in good order. Look after the details. Your objective is to get as fluent at what you do as you are in your own mother tongue—to attain mastery.

How do you go about doing a job with real mastery, if you're not a master of it yet? One suggestion that Tim Gallwey sometimes makes is to learn mastery by acting like a master. Imagine you're an old-timer. Pretend you really know the ropes. Do the job as if you were already a master. There's a confidence you can get from acting "as if" that can take you a surprising distance in a short time.

• Your Life Depends on It:

When the zen master Dogen was teaching his students how to cook, he told them, "Keep your wits about you. Wash the rice thoroughly, and don't lose even a single grain. Put the rice in the pot, light the fire, and let it cook. Don't allow it to boil over. There's an old saying: 'See the pot as your own head, see the water as your own blood.'"

In other words, do your work as if your life depended on it. To attain mastery is possible in any profession, but it requires that you be aware of what you're doing at all times. Ernie in the mailroom didn't waste an inch of string.

In the end, the real excellence of your work will depend on who or what you feel you are working for. As we saw in our analysis of the three major forms of work satisfaction, work that is done "to make a positive contribution" is complete in a way that other work is not.

People have aims, ideals, dreams; call them what you will. Everyone is "shooting for a target beyond the horizon" in some sense, whether their name for the target is God or Utopia, One World or the pleasure of the human heart. You can further increase your work satisfaction by dedicating your work; considering it an offering toward a higher goal.

You can make a small ritual out of your dedication. People dedicate the books they write, and there's no reason why you shouldn't dedicate your own work. Dedicate each piece of work to your family, or world peace, or whatever, and it will give you an additional reason to strive for excellence.

In India, this approach to work is called karma yoga. The strategy is simply to care as you work; to care about your work until your work becomes a gift of yourself.

The satisfaction that comes with this type of dedication is the kind after which you don't need books such as this. You are too busy doing, living, and feeling good. And this kind of satisfaction, finally, provides you with one last secret: you come to realize that it isn't what you do but your sense of being as you do it that matters.

● When All Else Fails:

This chapter has introduced a number of techniques for improving a boring or overwhelming situation by improving the way you deal with the work. But if you've tried everything and nothing has budged an inch in your favor, let's be frank about it: you can always quit.

If you can't find enough in this chapter to help you get through the job and grow in it, do yourself what may be a painful favor, and find other work where you can learn and grow.

## ZEN GOES FURTHER

The zen tradition takes its approach to work a lot further than this chapter, partly because zen students work as part of their study of zen—and are therefore willing to throw themselves into the process with abandon.

What more does zen have to say about work?

Zen teaches that the best work is done without strain, as if you had no goal in mind. It's an idea that comes close to Tim Gallwey's emphasis on effortless success, and it's the natural result of real, unworried absorption in your work.

Some years ago, there was a TV special about the monks in a zen monastery in Japan. One shot from that show stands out vividly. It was a shot of a zen monk, sweeping up snow in the monastery garden as the snow was still falling.

The monk wasn't stupid; he wasn't hoping to get rid of the snow. He wasn't hoping to sweep enough of it away that the rest would be easy to shovel up when the snowing stopped. He wasn't doing it because it was on the schedule, or because someone else told him to. He was doing it for another reason altogether.

He was doing it to be doing it. Because it didn't matter. He was doing it with what zen books call "purposeless purpose." It was so simple: his being was in his action. And somehow, that made it matter most of all.

He was sweeping the snow, to put it in more poetic terms, "because it's always snowing." Because the task is never finished. Because there's always more than can be done. Because life goes on.

# UNDERWRITING YOUR TRUE WORK

**Relevance:**    Particularly important for those who are planning to leave their current job to "go independent," also for artists, hobbyists, volunteers, and students who are paying their way through school.

**Premise:**    It is vitally important to be clear about goals, and continuously monitor progress to ensure that your dream keeps coming closer to reality.

**Strategy:**    Become professional about your dream. Underwrite the project you really care about by working simultaneously at another, better paying job.

**Tactics:**    Planning, implementation, and evaluation of both your paying work and your project; effective management of time, money, energy, and other resources.

# Chapter 7

# UNDERWRITING YOUR TRUE WORK

*If you don't want to work you have to work to earn
enough money so that you won't have to work.*

*Ogden Nash*

"I work in an office all day," Kelly told us, "and when I get
home, I often find myself giving in to voices in my head that say,
'Who are you kidding? You're not a songwriter, you're a mid-
level administrator.' And then there's fatigue. It's a struggle to
sit down at the piano instead of just relaxing with my friends or
watching TV. When I do sit down, though, and begin to play
something—anything at first, just to get myself going—it's a
real motivating factor. Just the process of doing it is all the
inspiration I need."

## UNDERWRITING

It is often possible to "underwrite" an important project by
paying your way working at a job that has little intrinsic interest,
and doing your project on the side. Kelly is underwriting her
music by working in an office.

Even when you have been "zenning it" in your paid job, you
may still feel that you have a deeper calling which needs to be
heard. Underwriting is one way that you can respond to it. You
will certainly be in good company. Louis Armstrong supported

himself by driving a coal delivery wagon while he was getting his start as a jazz trumpeter. Albert Einstein worked for years as a clerk in a patents office while he was preparing his great papers on statistical mechanics, the photoelectric effect, and the special theory of relativity. Millions of less known people have made a decision to work in this way.

- Personal Entrepreneurship:

The strategy of underwriting involves a kind of personal entrepreneurship. You are investing your time and effort (and very probably some capital) in the development of a project that you really want to do.

This may or may not be a business, but it is the dream in which you are hoping to find your satisfaction. With that much of yourself invested in it, you need to be as practical about it as you would be about starting a business in your spare time. All too frequently, it is done without much serious thought, and the results are often less than satisfactory. The purpose of this chapter, then, is to help you professionalize your dream.

You are the entrepreneur here, the realistic dreamer. You may think of your project as a hobby, an avocation, or a part-time interest. You may feel that because it is unpaid, it doesn't count as work. But in the sense that Picasso talked about, it is your "work in life," and you don't want to give it less than your best.

When you are involved in underwriting, three factors—money, time, and vitality—are essential. Without them, your project will never get off the ground. The greatest pitfall is the danger of kidding yourself that you are progressing when you are too poor, too busy, or too exhausted to be making any actual progress. Specifically, you need to make sure you don't fool yourself, or you'll wind up filling your life with broken promises, not totally committed to your paid job, and not moving forward with your deeper goals.

You need to know:

— whether you are underwriting on a temporary basis, or whether you will be doing it permanently.

— how you are going to motivate yourself when your underwriting job seems tedious or frustrating.

— how to set your goals, plan your course of action, put it into operation, and evaluate the results.

— how to manage your time, energy, and resources so that your underwriting will have the best chance of success.

— how to determine when, if ever, to cross over from underwriting into full-time work on your project.

These are the topics this chapter will address.

## LEADING A DOUBLE LIFE

If you are going to be underwriting your dream by working a "regular" job, you'll be doing what others would consider almost two full-time jobs. Effectively, you'll be leading a double life. And though you may be fresh when you start the first forty hours, you need to be equally fresh when you begin your second project.

If you have chosen to lead this kind of double life, you must recognize that there will always be activities, chores, and social events that you won't have as much time for as do those who are leading "singular" lives. For a parent who is responsible for the primary care of children, finding the time to spend on the project is likely to be even tougher. If you can't get to your dream for years at a stretch, keep it alive any way you can, even if that means just promising yourself over and over that you'll get back to it when your last child gets into grade school.

Underwriting is a tough challenge. Give yourself credit for

being ambitious, dedicated, and self-motivated. If you weren't, you wouldn't be attempting this balancing act in the first place.

• Choosing Your Underwriting Strategies:

Let's assume for the moment that you know what your dream project will be. You have a choice as to how you will underwrite it. What should you consider as you choose the job that will support you while you work on your project?

It may be helpful to pick a job that is related to your true goal. The closer your underwriting job is to your "real" vocation, the easier it will be for the motivation from one to pass over into the other. Furthermore, skills learned in one place can then be transferred to the other.

Cindy hopes to become a full-time employee of the children's museum where she currently volunteers her time. Meanwhile, her closely related job as a substitute teacher gives her plenty of opportunity to work with children.

On the other hand many people, and many artists in particular, have found that working "too close to the vein" deprives them of their creative energy in the very area where it is most essential. An underwriting job that relates to your dream may pay more and may be more congenial than one that's not related to your special interest, but it may also crowd out your dream.

Mitch works as a waiter precisely for that reason. When he leaves the restaurant, that's it. He doesn't have to carry his work home; his mind is free to concentrate on writing. And, as he also admits, some of the characters he serves find their way into his stories.

Everyone must discover what works best for them in this area.

There is another choice that may confront you if you are adopting an underwriting strategy. Are you working toward a time when you will be able to devote yourself full-time to your project, or not?

- Temporary Underwriting:

Some people need only underwrite their chosen work for a while, before they accumulate enough capital or education to proceed with their career plans. It's clear to them that waiting on tables or painting houses will pay off in the end, that they'll finish their computer courses at night, and get the job they really want as a systems analyst.

Those who are engaged in temporary underwriting may not have to worry about having enough time and energy to work simultaneously on their dream if they can manage to make progress toward it. Temporary underwriting work need have very little to do with your specific talents and interests: what is important is that it contribute to your final goal.

Even a very tough job (working an island lighthouse in isolation and heavy weather for a year) if it pays well enough, can justify itself by eventually allowing you to do what you really want.

On the other hand, if you work at a well-paying job that you hate in order to save up enough to do a project of your own, and then spend all your earnings in an effort to find the satisfaction your job doesn't bring you—no progress is being made.

Another advantage of temporary underwriting is that you know you won't have to do it forever. Underwriting jobs that would be intolerable if you had to do them indefinitely can be lived through when you know they're going to be over soon.

The following story illustrates one successful application of the temporary underwriting strategy.

On October 15, 1978, an all-women team of mountaineers made the first women's ascent of Annapurna, one of only fourteen 8,000-meter mountains in the world. To get there, the team members not only had to make all the usual preparations for a major climb; they had also set up a T-shirt business to underwrite their project.

The idea for the climb arose in 1972 when Arlene Blum, the team leader, met a Polish climber, Wanda Rutkiewicz, coming down from the summit of Noshaq, a 7,000-meter peak in Afghanistan. At the time, no woman had climbed any of the world's 8,000-meter peaks, and Rutkiewicz and Blum determined to be the first.

In 1973, they applied to the Nepalese government for permission to climb Annapurna, and were turned down. In the meantime, women from Japan, China and Poland climbed 8,000-meter peaks, and Blum herself was a member of an American Everest team, climbing to 7,467 meters. But the lure of Annapurna, and the idea of making an ascent with an all-woman expedition, remained.

In 1978, the goal was achieved, despite the deaths of two members in the second team. The American Women's Himalayan Expedition (AWHE) became the fifth party to climb Annapurna, the first Americans, and the first expedition of women to do so.

Mountaineering is an expensive business. In order to raise the $80,000 that the climb would cost, the AWHE not only received funding from the National Geographic Society, they also went into business and sold 10,000 T-shirts with the motto "A woman's place is on top: Annapurna."

The women of AWHE knew from the beginning that their underwriting strategy was a temporary one. They weren't in the T-shirt business, even when they went about the business of selling T-shirts: they were in the Annapurna business, and T-shirts were the means to an end.

● Time to Switch:

If your underwriting strategy is a temporary one, it is important that you have some way of determining when you have arrived at the crossover point, and can switch full-time to your chosen profession. You'll need to set yourself a time frame and write down some criteria that will let you know when you're ready for the change. These criteria need to include issues of time and money, but they may also include elements such as the acquisition of skills, experience, credentials, and the right contacts.

Spending your entire life getting the capital together for a venture you'll never get around to isn't underwriting. It's all the hard work of underwriting, and none of the benefits.

There are two rules here, and they face (as so often in real life) in opposite directions:

1. Don't expect too much too soon. Be prepared to work, and wait, and be patient. Successful underwriting takes time, effort, common sense, and uncommon enthusiasm.

2. Don't wait too long. If you're not making any headway toward your real goals, you aren't underwriting, you're kidding yourself.

It may help you to think in terms of a gradual shift in your activities, rather than a single crossover point. The important thing is to approach this business intelligently and conservatively. Many business people, for instance, begin consulting for private clients on the side before they start their own consulting firms. Writers, photographers, and graphic designers can often pick up freelance work while they are still employed at their soon-to-be-previous jobs. Doing paid part-time work on your project, while you are finishing up your underwriting career, is one way to make the crossover smoother.

● Permanent Underwriting:

Some people know that they will never be able to switch over full-time to the work they love. They understand that their pet project will never pay for itself. This situation crops up most often in the arts and in the area of community service.

Jody Dickerson has a successful dental practice in New Orleans. His is a highly professional, full-time occupation, but Jody views it as a means of underwriting his real passion: jazz piano. One of the reasons he went into dentistry was to be financially able to play an active role as a pianist in the New Orleans jazz scene, and to build himself a studio to record his compositions.

If you realize that you're going to be underwriting permanently, you may decide that you need to place considerable emphasis on career development in both your paid job and the project you're underwriting. What does it look like when you've managed this strategy so well that you're a highly successful professional in two fields?

John Safer is an artist whose bronzes and Plexiglas sculptures have been bought by museums and private collectors. He is also chairman of the board of the District of Columbia National Bank.

Perhaps Safer wouldn't describe his banking as "underwriting" his sculpture. He's someone who has managed to find success in two very different careers, and he takes delight in them both. He does acknowledge, though, that the motivations and satisfactions of the two areas are very different. "You enter a business venture for profit or acclaim or excitement or for a half-dozen other reasons," he told the *Harvard Business Review* in a recent interview. "You create a work of art because you must. This is the key. I find it difficult to take anything in life very seriously . . . but somehow a work of art seems to rise a little above the rest of human achievement."

Ted Weller is another example of the wide variety of ways in which one can find work that is compatible with one's dream. Weller has been working for some years collecting material for a dictionary of clichés and their origins. It's a lifetime project, one that involves reading widely in classical and contemporary literature, and organizing a vast index of quotations.

He can't make a living at this project, now or in the foreseeable future. But the secondhand bookstore Weller owns pays his bills, and keeps a steady flow of material coming his way. He enjoys the freedom of being his own boss, the opportunity to talk with collectors and students of literature, and the chance to find new treasures for his dictionary. Ted's a booklover—which isn't exactly a job-description or a life's work. But he's managed to find a way to weave both his life's work (the dictionary) and his paid work (the bookstore) out of the same fabric.

What Ted Weller, Jody Dickerson, and John Safer have in common is that each of them has found a way to "take care of business" and also work on the projects they love.

What can you learn from these stories about the art of juggling a permanent paying job with an important second pursuit?

First, the paying job needs to pay. As John Safer says, banks are "where the money is." Creating bronze sculptures is hardly a low-cost endeavor. And Jody Dickerson's dental practice allows him to buy new recording equipment and travel to those concerts.

Second, your underwriting work needs to leave you with time to work on your personal project, and should feed into it if possible. Ted Weller's shop not only offers him times during the day to work on his dictionary, it also provides him with the materials he needs—a constant supply of books.

Third, even if your job doesn't directly relate to your project, it needs to be one that feels reasonably compatible. It can't be the sort that leaves you feeling drained at the end of a day.

● Making the Choice:

When it's time to decide whether your strategy should be one of temporary or permanent underwriting, ask yourself the following questions:

What do you aim to achieve by underwriting?

Do you need to change jobs, to strengthen the financial aspect of your underwriting strategy? To make sure enough time is available for your chosen project? To have enough vitality left at the end of the working day to make progress on your project?

• Finding Motivation:

Motivation may be a problem, particularly if you're working at a job you don't too much like in order to support the work you really want to do. How can you motivate yourself to do the paid job so you can underwrite your project? You'll unquestionably want to take advantage of the tactics discussed in the previous chapter, "Zenning It." But what if your paid job gets boring or frustrating, and nothing you learned about "zenning it" seems to be working for you at the moment? You need to remind yourself that what you're doing is underwriting.

Many people who are working at less than satisfying jobs in order to pursue work that is "more their cup of tea" tend to focus on all the ways in which the less satisfactory work is blocking the more important stuff. They become frustrated, and usually run out of enthusiasm for the paying job.

The motivation to succeed at a job that is not your "true" work, but which pays for it, must come from knowing that it is empowering you to achieve your goals. You need to use your true work as a means of vitalizing your attitude toward your paid work.

Phil's story illustrates some specific techniques that can help you do this. Phil has been gathering momentum in the insurance business for some time. First, he was a junior underwriter of homeowner policies. Then, as a group pension technician, he determined the benefits to be paid to people covered under group pension policies. His next job as a customer relations representative involved increased responsibility: he still underwrote policies, but was now also negotiating conflicts between his company and policy holders. Most recently, Phil has landed a job providing insurance expertise to the in-house programming department of another company, helping to create new software that meets the company's specific needs.

Phil's progress has been ordered and consistent. His work is satisfactory at the first level: it pays his way. But it isn't his dream. Indeed, Phil has an entirely separate career as a musician. He has played clarinet under such distinguished conductors as Aaron Copeland and Pinchas Zuckerman. He is clear in his own mind that his real calling is the performance and teaching of classical music. He's waiting and working for his break, the audition that will bring him an orchestral chair.

How does he feel about insurance? Sometimes good, and sometimes terrible. But whenever his job is getting him down, it's the realization that he's working towards that orchestral seat that carries him through. Our advice to Phil was that he should do "target practice." The idea here is to "target" the work that you want to underwrite through the "sights" of the work you're doing to underwrite it.

We suggested to Phil that he keep music in his sights when he was working at his insurance job. Then Phil had a stroke of luck. He found a full-page ad for the local Philharmonic orchestra in the newspaper, with a headline which read: "Phil your life with Music." Perfect. He cut it out, framed it, and keeps it on his desk. When Phil feels stuck in his insurance work, he looks at that advertisement. He brings his target motivation (music) in line with his sights (the work before him). And he remembers why he took the job in the first place.

## THE ESSENCE OF MANAGEMENT

If you're going to underwrite your dream, you need to be professional about it. The major management skills you'll want to develop are in the areas of time, money, and energy. You need to be efficient enough in managing your paying job that you are free to pursue your project, and efficient enough at managing your project to make sure that it gets done.

The essence of time management lies in three words: planning, doing, and evaluating. Knowing what is most important, having the discipline to pursue it, and evaluating your results are the keys to success.

- Planning:

Planning is designed to ensure that you do as much as possible with whatever resources you possess. Effective planning includes the following procedures:

— becoming clear on your long-range goals;

— mapping the route you will take to reach them;

— setting short-term goals; and

— scheduling.

Woven in with these time-oriented procedures, you will also need to take care of:

— budgeting, and

— beating exhaustion.

It's the true business of your life that you're planning. You want to be as serious about this as you would be about running a business; and that means writing your plans and projections down, and evaluating your progress as you go along.

- Long-range Goals:

All planning begins with your long-range goals. You have already begun the process of clarifying what these goals are, by clarifying your values in the first part of this book, and by deciding whether you fall into the temporary or permanent underwriting category.

— What are your long-term goals for the project you want to underwrite? And for the work you're going to do to underwrite it?

— What would be the usual steps to take, to arrive at your long-term "paid work" goals?

— What would be another way of going about things?

— What would be the usual steps to take, to arrive at your long-term "dream project" goals?

— What would be another way of going about things?

When you know what your underwriting goals are, you need to map out your overall approach to these long-term goals. List the major steps involved in each of these approaches, both to your paid work and to your project. Since your project represents something of a dream, it may be appropriate to adopt an innovative strategy for going about it. But what about the work you will do to underwrite it? Your underwriting work needs, above all, to proceed smoothly and efficiently. You may find the conventional, step-by-step approach is most appropriate here.

As soon as you have a sense of the path you're going to take, you need to make a plan of the major stages, including some rough deadlines for accomplishing these steps.

• Critical Path Analysis:

There's a simple principle that you can use to help your planning be more effective. It's called critical path analysis. Sophisticated computerized versions of critical path analysis are used in business management under such names as CPM (Critical Path Method) and PERT (Program Evaluation and Review Technique). The principles are applicable to any level of planning. The basic idea is to plan backwards from the results you intend to achieve.

Making a critical path analysis involves drawing up a plan which shows you every major step you'll need to take to bring your project to completion. As you make your plan, you'll find that some things have to be finished before others can be begun, others can be accomplished simultaneously, and some can be incorporated whenever there's a spare moment.

When you have planned for each stage that needs to be accomplished, and calculated the time that each one will take, you'll see that one particular series of processes necessarily takes the longest time to complete. That's known as your critical path.

Your aim should be to shorten this longest path, which you can manage by getting as many things as possible to happen simultaneously. When you have worked out the tightest version of this critical path, you need to translate it into a schedule. This schedule will let you know what has to be done by when, if your final goal is to be accomplished on time.

Your critical path analysis gives you information about what's possible. You will get a clear sense of the earliest possible starting date for any particular activity, and its earliest finishing date. You will also learn the latest date on which to start each stage of the process, and the latest date on which that part can be completed and still maintain your overall schedule.

The sliding room between these earliest and latest dates is called your "float." It's important to remember that when you use up some of your float in one activity, it may have implications for the amount of float available to you elsewhere.

This planning technique has a number of advantages. To accomplish it, you will have to clearly visualize the entire process from beginning to end. You will be forced to ask yourself a number of questions about the project that would have come up anyway, but perhaps too late for you to deal with them successfully. Above all, you will have considerably added to your clarity, and hence your motivation.

Critical path analysis can be applied to something as complex as building a house, or something as simple as making sure you've whittled down the balance owing on your credit card in time to use it to buy the cheaper fare ticket two weeks before you want to fly. When the project is a complex one, you'll need the whole apparatus of initial planning, identifying the critical path, shortening it, noting the important time frames, and so on. But even in simple cases, just working backwards from your goal through its various subgoals can sometimes save you endless frustration.

Here's an example of how to go about it:

Judy lives in the Midwest, and is passionate about square dancing and horses. She decided several years ago that she wanted to leave her job as a legal secretary and open a western clothing store. She knew she was planning to make a big jump, and she prepared for it carefully.

Four years have passed, and Judy has long since left the small town lawyer's office. She went to night school at her local community college for a year, and took classes in bookkeeping and small business management. She took a cut in pay, and worked for a while as a salesperson in a local department store, then joined their buyer training program and worked for a year as a buyer. After that she moved to the city where she wanted to start her business.

Just before she moved, Judy visualized the things she'd need before she could open The Pony Express for its first day of business. She'd need staff. She'd need the actual store site. She'd need it decorated to her taste. And she'd need an inventory of everything from Levis and Stetsons to tack.

She began to work back from there, and when she was through filling in the major time-lines, this was the plan she came up with:

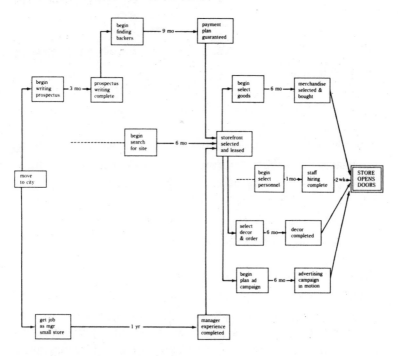

Judy's plan underwent some alterations and revisions as she made progress towards her goal, of course. But the very act of planning gave her invaluable insights about the process she would be undertaking.

● Setting Short-term Goals:

There's no need to set out your short-term steps all the way to the final achievement of your life's goal. But your next month's aims and objectives needs to be generally defined, this month's objectives need to be known, and this week's tasks need to be in clear focus. Ask yourself:

— What are your objectives for the next two months, in terms of your project? In terms of your paid job?

— What are your objectives for this month?

— What are you doing about it this week?

**146**

The best-laid plans, etcetera. You need to take a look at each of the steps you have outlined, and make allowances for the unpredictable. You need to plan on the unplannable. It sounds both practical and ridiculous, and it is; utterly ridiculous, and extremely practical.

— What sorts of problems are likely to arise at each step along the way?

— How could you deal with these contingencies?

— How long might this take?

● Scheduling:

Scheduling is the detailed planning in the short-term that corresponds to critical path analysis over the long run. It lets you know the next step at any given point. The rules are simple and obvious, and almost nobody follows them. Those who do follow them succeed much more often than those who don't.

Start each day by drawing up a total list of the tasks you hope to accomplish today. Include any tasks you didn't get to yesterday, or left incomplete, as well as any meetings you already have on your schedule.

Now screen your task list. Ask yourself the following questions:

— Which tasks simply have to be done today?

— Which tasks can be done later?

— Which tasks could you ask someone else to do?

— Which tasks might be postponed indefinitely?

— How long will today's tasks realistically take, including an extra 15 percent for contigencies?

— What details have been left sitting around and need to be cleaned up before they are totally forgotten?

— Which of your tasks would it delight you to accomplish?

You should be able to run through this procedure in about five minutes, and then schedule your day around the most important items.

• Financial Planning:

You need to manage money wisely if you are going to make enough to live on and still have enough left over to finance your dream project. The skills you need here are prioritization and discipline. You need to know how important your various goals are to you, and to make financial priorities that will allow you to get on with your project. That may mean cutting back on other areas of your life. It may also mean recognizing that those other areas are equally important to you, and changing the definition of your dream. In either case, it involves getting a clearer picture of what you really want.

Doing financial planning, holding to your proposed budget, and keeping good books are all necessary to ensure that money isn't what blocks you from your dream. If you are drawing up a critical path plan, whether simple or complex, one of the factors you will certainly include is money. Money has its deadlines just as all the other factors in a critical path analysis do. Perhaps more than any other factor, lack of money can capsize an underwriting venture.

There are numerous books on the market that deal with personal goal-setting, time management, and money management. These are all large subjects in themselves, and this book has simply tried to touch on the most important points. If you feel you need more help, pick the books that appeal to you from the list in the appendix, and apply their techniques to your situation. Your "work in life" is at stake.

## DOING

When you've taken care of planning in both the long- and short-term, you need to make sure you complete the tasks you have scheduled. There's nothing particularly glamorous about it: it's a matter of plugging away until you've done the job.

A now-successful science fiction writer sent off 300 submissions to magazines before his first two stories were accepted. Even an excellent first science fiction novel, which takes perhaps a year to write, will often sell for as little as $2,000. Bill had to keep working at his office job, writing promotional literature, while he was sending all those stories out.

But he sent them. He would mail a batch of five stories every two weeks. When a story came back with a rejection slip, he simply made a notation in his card file, turned the manuscript around and mailed it out to another magazine. In addition, he kept writing new and better stories so that he could retire the old ones. Plugging away at his project brought Bill eventual success.

As usual, the most important things that can be said in this area are matters of common sense. Determination and a few simple rules can take you a long way. Be punctual, and keep the promises you make to yourself. They are promises you made because they would help you achieve your goals, and failure to keep them is a form of self-betrayal. Whole books have been written about doing, but everything that can be said on the subject is a platitude. In the end, it all boils down to one thing: either you do, or you don't.

## EVALUATION

Evaluation is the final stage in the management of any long- or short-term goals. It's the point at which you see what you have and haven't done, honestly, clearly, and with a minimum of praise or blame. That last phrase may seem surprising: but blame can knot your stomach as surely as praise can go to your head. And neither one of them makes it easy for you to learn, to improve, and to carry right on.

You will want to critique your progress toward your various long- and short-term goals, using the time lines you devised during the planning process.

— Did you come out on target?

— What did you learn from what you did?

— What course corrections do you need to make?

— How should your next planning session reflect what you have learned?

Finally, if you find yourself running into a crisis, ask yourself how much you contributed to the situation that led to it, and what you can do to make things run more smoothly next time.

## LIFE MANAGEMENT

Your life energy or vitality is the third and most important of the three kinds of energy you have at your disposal; and it's the one that you can't plan in advance. It's something you have to monitor all the time, while you're actually out doing the things you've planned. It's very easy for your underwriting job to leave you too exhausted to work on your real project. Here are some ways to go about the process of conservation of energy.

Be patient. Patience is bound to be an important attitude for those who are underwriting their dream. Indeed, the whole secret of underwriting is often summed up in one word: waiting. A large number of people literally spend the time until their crossover point arrives waiting—on tables. There are probably enough Ph.D.'s waiting tables in most of the larger American cities to provide the core faculty for a college or two.

Be impatient, too. Having patience is essential to most underwriting. But impatience can also play its part by finally driving you to the work you've always wanted. One way to express yourself clearly is to learn to say "no" to others so that you can say "yes" to your dream. Having the patience to wait things out without getting overly frustrated, coupled with a healthy ability to let your frustration motivate you, can take you a long way. The trick is finding a balance of the two, and not getting stuck exclusively in either.

Be honest with yourself. Many people finally discover that the main factor holding them back from their dream is fear: fear of failure, and perhaps a little fear of success too. Let yourself know what's holding you back, and you'll already have won half the battle. As long as the fear is covered up, there is very little that can be done about it; once it is recognized, it won't seem nearly as overwhelming. Nothing frees up your energy as much as getting beyond your doubts and fears.

Stay informed about any tools that are available to help with your project. Jonathan didn't know there were tools available for stripping the layers of old linoleum from hardwood floors until he'd almost finished his "dream project" of renovating a Victorian house. As he told us with a slightly wry grin, "I finally realized that there's a tool for virtually everything."

Keep informed about people, too. Find out what networks already exist that have to do with your dream. Computer users' groups can put you in touch with free software. Fellow artists may be able to offer suggestions about how to market your paintings or prints. And so on.

Seek productive relationships. If you can find someone who has a dream project that's similar to yours, offer to work with them on their project in return for help with your own. Just bouncing ideas back and forth with someone who's interested in the same area can release tremendous amounts of creative energy. Working together on joint projects can be a fine way to start up and maintain a deep friendship.

Don't be hesitant to look for help when you need it. When you meet someone who has pulled off the very thing that you want to achieve, take advantage of your opportunity. Explain your situation, and listen carefully to what they have to say. Ask for enough clarity to cut through exaggerated hopes, and enough encouragement to propel you toward your goal.

Don't be afraid to go to the top. A well-written, interesting "help" letter from a beginner is irresistible; and a successful person will often find time to meet with someone who shares their dream.

## YOU ARE YOUR OWN BOSS

In the process of underwriting, you are both boss and employee. What kind of boss are you? How do you, as an employee, feel about working for yourself? What changes would you like to see in yourself as a boss? What kind of employee are you? How would you feel, as a boss, about hiring yourself to get your project accomplished? What changes would you like to see in yourself as an employee?

Like any other boss, you need to make sure that things get done. And like any employee, you need to survive the job. You're (both) in an ideal bargaining position, and can surely work something out together.

Remember, you are ultimately answerable only to yourself. You will need to be both realistic and idealistic about this. If you are leading the "double life," you can hardly overestimate the importance of not kidding yourself. There's a tremendous amount of satisfaction in the process of going for what you want, and a great deal more in achieving it.

# LEARNING AND CHANGING

**Relevance:**   Particularly helpful for those who have to keep pace with new developments in the workplace; and for those who want to learn either to make their present job more interesting, or to upgrade their skills.

**Premise:**   Learning can be a major source of satisfaction; it is also an essential skill for dealing successfully with rapid change.

**Strategy:**   To develop areas of true expertise, continually introduce yourself to areas that are completely new, both on and off the job.

**Tactics:**   Developing the learning attitude; choosing what you want to learn; job-related trainings; learning from a mentor; and acquiring general business and interpersonal skills.

# Chapter 8

---

# LEARNING AND CHANGING

*Anyone who keeps learning stays young.*
                                        *Henry Ford*

Diane works for one of the top auditing firms in the country. Her first love was always singing, and she majored in voice at college; she also earned a teaching credential in music education as a backup. She taught music to elementary school children until the taxpayers in her state voted a budget cut, and the funding for her job suddenly dried up. She could type, so she got a job as a secretary at the auditing company.

In the course of five years, with no formal background in accounting, she learned her way up the ladder. Diane is now an assistant auditor, and earns far more than she would ever have earned as a teacher. In addition, Diane successfully underwrites her dream of singing choral and operatic music.

## THE LEARNING DIFFERENCE

This chapter is about learning—what it can do for you, what attitudes will help you learn successfully, and most importantly, what learning options are available to you.

Learning may sound like a straightforward matter of adding

to one's store of skills. It is, and it can also be not only a major source of satisfaction, but an inexhaustible way to increase your enjoyment of even a dull job. It is a crucial element in any successful strategy for dealing with rapid change.

Every job is an incredible learning opportunity, and there is little which is as delightful for some, or so useful to others, as continual learning. When learning is forced on us (as it often is in school), it can be traumatic. But when we consciously choose to learn, the experience is almost always immensely rewarding.

## WHAT LEARNING CAN DO FOR YOU

Most people know that physical exercise is beneficial—that it strengthens the heart, improves digestion, increases your chance of longevity, deepens your sleep, and helps you cope with stress. All the same, it's good to be reminded of these things from time to time. What are the benefits of learning?

— Learning is to the mind what exercise is to the body: it keeps you in shape so that you can stretch when you need to.

— Learning means that you don't get left behind when the world changes; it helps you keep up with new technologies, both in your own field and in others.

— Learning makes your world more interesting, and makes you more interesting, too.

— Learning develops your existing skills, provides you with new ones, and allows you to discover abilities you didn't know you possessed.

— Learning increases your options; it gives you the ability to create choices, rather than being limited by what the system offers.

— Learning can be a lifelong process, with lifelong rewards.

— Learning can make an otherwise boring job interesting and satisfying.


● Trial and Error versus Tried and True:

In times of rapid change, learning is the key ability that allows us to adapt to new and different circumstances. The greater the rate of change, the more important this ability becomes.

Change means that the "tried and true" works less and less often, and so we are forced back to the creative experimental method that provided our predecessors with those "tried" truths in the first place—trial and error. As the very phrase "trial and error" suggests, mistakes will be a part of this process. We must constantly "go back to the drawing board" and rethink our way of doing almost everything.

In times of change, we must be able to survive when the tried and true ways no longer work. In fact, changes are now taking place so rapidly in all aspects of our society that we need to practice dealing with change itself; we need to become expert learners.

Thomas J. Watson, the founder of IBM, put it this way: "To succeed, double your failure rate." Real success lies in the ability to get right what you got wrong once before. Successful people aren't those who never take risks and never make mistakes. They are the people who build on their mistakes, who learn from them, who regard their errors as the soil from which success can grow.

Thomas Watson really meant it when he said "double your failure rate." He wasn't just paying lip service to the idea. The story goes that he once called an IBM executive who had just made a mistake that cost the company $10 million into his office. The two of them talked about what had happened, and at the end of the meeting the executive asked Watson, "Aren't you going to fire me?" "How can I fire you, now that I've just spent $10 million educating you?" Watson asked.

● Learning Gives You Confidence:

Learning offers you new insights, methods, styles, and solutions. It offers you possibilities where before you saw impossibilities, and choices where you had no choices. People feel bored and frustrated when they have only one choice. Learning is the opposite of boredom: it is the essence of freedom of choice.

Those who have mastered the new technology, the new procedure, the new language, or whatever, are not only better prepared for the workplace, they are also more confident in general. They have achieved a breakthrough: the unknown has become known.

Lynn had an accident at work. Workmen's Compensation insurance covered her medical expenses, but at the end of six months it became clear that she wouldn't be able to return to her old job. The insurance also paid for Lynn to go through a battery of aptitude tests to help her determine what field she could retrain in, and one of their strongly weighted suggestions was that she might try computer programming.

This was an area that Lynn had never considered. She had always been terrible at math, and had therefore assumed that computers weren't right for her. But Lynn was willing to give it a try. She wound up in an "intensified learning" computer school. She hadn't been a student in over fifteen years, and she was terrified. She was worried she wouldn't be able to learn the material, that she couldn't keep up. She spent one entire class quietly crying in the back of the room. Finally, something broke, and she realized she had "cried herself out."

From that moment on, Lynn wasn't working against herself any longer. The programming languages finally started to make sense. But it wasn't until she received an "A" on the first test in each of her classes that she knew for sure she could make it through school. She realized she could make it through anything; and that if her circumstances changed all over again, she could still make it.

Learning not only increases your confidence by increasing your abilities, it also rubs off in the form of a general attitude to life: that problems can be solved, difficulties can be overcome, fears can be diminished, and that more things are possible than you imagined.

## LEARNING THE LEARNING ATTITUDE

The ability to learn is an ability that everyone possesses. It is also an ability that you can significantly develop by cultivating those qualities which facilitate learning.

First, you need a willingness to learn. To gain new information, the two most useful phrases in the language are "I don't know" and "Can you help me?" Don't underestimate them. Those who "know it all" never learn, precisely because it doesn't occur to them to ask.

Learning happens when you are curious and inquisitive. Curiosity means asking yourself question after question, particularly about those things that seem obvious and which you tend to take for granted. You must question your own opinions, ideas, and assumptions. It's often useful to ask yourself the following questions: "What seems to be going on here? What's really happening? Why? What could make things better? How can I accomplish that?" The idea is to come to grips with the realities that underly our commonplace assumptions, and to find ways to cope with facts that don't fit into our accustomed picture of what's going on. These new insights often lead to innovative strategies —and awards for the suggestions you drop in the box.

The ability to question others is also crucial to success. You need to be able to question others in such a way that you come to a clear understanding of what they want to communicate. One useful entrepreneurial skill is the ability to ask questions in such a way that you don't suggest the reply you want. This involves the ability to hold back your own opinions and listen to the other person's answer. Finding the kinds of questions that provoke interesting answers is important: "What makes things hardest for you in your business?" "What is the next development in your field that will set it on its ear?" "What does your competitor (or the leading company in the field) do better than your company?" "What is your company's greatest potential strength?"

Real listening involves respecting the other person's right to an opinion, and people who listen well are listened to willingly. You can learn both how to ask questions and how to listen carefully by watching an interviewer like Phil Donahue. His questions open up the subject area he's interested in; but once his interviewee gets going, he's alert and attentive to what they want to say, and uses further questions to zero in more precisely on the hints and clues they provide. As an interviewer, he's first and foremost a good listener.

The abilities to question and to listen, taken together, add up to the ability to get willing cooperation from others. An enormous amount of job satisfaction comes from being able to communicate effectively with people who feel they can communicate with you.

Learning also requires determination and follow through. But gritting your teeth and trying too hard seldom works. Learning happens best when it's allowed to, not when it's forced.

When serious thinking has failed to solve a problem or understand the impact of a new situation, playfulness often helps. "When we hire new people, we're not so concerned with how intelligent or efficient they are," the president of a microprocessor company admitted recently. "To us, the important characteristics are their playfulness and their intensity." The willingness to make mistakes, to seem foolish, is one of the great clues to learning. Learning happens when you take risks. The "fool" who "persists in his folly and becomes wise" soon finds himself with a reputation for excellence.

When you acquire the learning attitude, you gain not only the ability to learn more, but also a set of skills that will make you more engaged in whatever you do, with productive results in your level of work satisfaction, your work and your life.

So far, you have looked at the value of learning, and the attitude on your part that it requires. It is time to take a look at what kinds of learning are available.

There are various ways to go about the business of learning. You can learn formally, by taking training, or informally, by means of curiosity and attentiveness. You can learn from people who have skills that you would like to develop. You can learn skills that are directly job-related, general business skills such as time management, budgeting, marketing, and promotion, and interpersonal skills such as diplomacy and the ability to negotiate. You can also learn skills and attitudes from your life experience that will help you in your place of work.

Make some resource lists as you read through the next few pages, so that you can begin to explore the various avenues that are applicable in your own circumstances. Each of the following sections will discuss different kinds of opportunities which may be open to you. In any section that applies to your situation, answer the questions in as much detail as you can, and make lists.

## LEARNING ON THE JOB

You can often receive formal training on the job to acquire skills that are useful or essential for your work. Usually this involves learning technical skills which will enable you to perform a particular task or use a new tool. Before you plan your learning program, there are a few questions you may want to ask yourself, or discuss with the company's personnel director, your boss, or your coworkers:

— What additional skills would be relevant in your present line of work? What skills or information do the people in a job you would like to be doing have?

— Is there job-related training offered at your place of work? Can you find someone who will teach you something you want to know?

— Does your company offer any paid, outside training?

— Will they contribute to the cost of a work-related study course?

— Are there companies in related areas that offer free training? Airlines offer training, for instance, to people who work for travel agencies.

— Are there opportunities for you to obtain credits toward a further degree, with tuition paid by your employer?

On-the-job training can not only be a rich source of job satisfaction in itself, it can also prepare you for new and more interesting work.

● Learning from a Mentor:

There's one highly personal and effective approach to on-the-job learning that you might seriously consider: acquiring a mentor.

Linda Phillips-Jones, a management and career development consultant and researcher for the American Institutes for Research of Palo Alto, California, defines a mentor as "an individual who goes out of his or her way to do something significant to help you reach your life goals."

The idea of a mentor is a very old one, and by no means confined to the realm of business. In the Middle Ages, skills in the various craft guilds were passed down from master to apprentice. In more recent times, the tradition of a younger person assisting an older and more experienced one, and receiving personal training and assistance in return, has flourished.

The graduate student who helps his or her professor with research or teaching is an example of the institutionalization of this relationship. In the business world, companies such as Merrill Lynch and Hughes Aircraft have established formal mentor programs. No form of learning compares with watching an experienced pro at work. And there are few more enjoyable ways of learning than to receive training and encouragement from someone you admire.

Mentors are more usually found informally. The best way to go about finding a mentor is to identify someone near the top of your organization, possibly even in a different division, with whom you have the "right chemistry." Such a person can give you several kinds of help as you climb the organizational ladder. As Adele Scheele suggests in her book, *Skills for Success,* they will often "be able to foresee developments in our position before we do, perhaps because of privileged information regarding executive decisions, or because they can sense our strengths even before we do and can encourage us to take a big, new step, or they will introduce us to someone who will prove to be the next link in our advancing career."

How do you find a mentor if you work in a company that's so small you know everyone already, and there are no suitable candidates? One way is to join the appropriate professional organization and volunteer to work on a committee.

Jeff Salzman and James Califano, in their book, *Real World 101,* suggests that one should "court" a potential mentor. They emphasize that the mentor-protégé relationship is almost unique among working relationships in that it is primarily based on emotions. This emotional bonding is what powers the relationship between mentor and protégé. It gives the mentor a strong motivation to teach the protégé "the things they don't teach you at Harvard Business School," and also to give the protégé powerful patronage and assistance. The protégé, in turn, feels a very real sense of being appreciated, both as a human being and specifically in terms of their work.

This emotional bonding also has its disadvantages. The relationship between mentor and protégé is similar to that between parent and child, or lover and lover. It can turn sour, and if it does, both your life and your work prospects are bound to suffer.

Some people have bosses who also act as their mentors; as their boss gets promoted, they move up too. But there are risks involved in this procedure as well. Your boss is unlikely to want to lose one of his or her closest associates through promotion to an equivalent position to their own in another department.

Picking a mentor is one place where you need to be an excellent judge of character. The relationship is best initiated informally, perhaps while working on a joint project. It only works with the right person, at the right time. But because of the strongly emotional nature of the relationship, it's a form of learning that at its best can be particularly satisfying.

— Is finding a mentor an idea that might be right for you?

— Does your company offer a formal or informal mentor program?

— Do you know someone who you would like to approach about being your mentor? If not, how might you start to look for such a person?

• Volunteering Up:

Perhaps you can volunteer your way into training. You may even be able to volunteer your way into a new job. Most people simply don't realize how possible it can be to move from one part of an organization to another, by making it known in a diplomatic way that they would like to contribute to a different area of the company's effort.

Kay was working as a secretary in the publicity department of a publishing house when she decided that she'd rather work on the editing staff. She started her campaign by reading book manuscripts on her own time and coming to editorial meetings. When an opening occurred in the editorial department, she was not only among the first to hear about it, she was also the natural choice for the job. Kay effectively "volunteered herself up" into her more interesting (and better paid) job as an assistant editor.

— Is there another part of your company that you'd rather work for? If so, can you volunteer your way into it?

• Daily Learning:

There are also more informal ways to go about learning while you work. There are a number of skills and insights that can be learned, even at a job that's far from ideal. These skills can be picked up by being attentive, open-minded, and curious at work.

These skills include such things as how to write a good business letter, memo, or report; how to be more creative; how to run an effective meeting; how to make decisions and implement them; how to increase teamwork; how to deal with one's superiors; and how to make contacts and network effectively.

You don't necessarily have to be the person who does these things in order to learn them. You can pick up a great deal from watching and talking with other people. Of course, you will want to learn from people who do these things really well; but you can also learn an enormous amount by seeing people do them badly. Remember, too, that you can learn things from people whose style is very different from your own, perhaps even from people you don't personally enjoy.

We often learn more than we realize by "picking things up" as we go along. To help you to recognize how much learning actually goes on in your work, make a careful list of your answers to the next few questions.

— What skills have you learned by watching other people?

— Could some of the skills you've learned at work be used in another context?

— What information have you gained by these informal methods?

— What contacts have you made that are of professional use to you?

— What have you learned on the job that might be useful in the rest of your life?

The more you recognize both what you have learned and the wide variety of ways in which the learning occurs, the readier you will be to take full advantage of other learning situations. That readiness translates directly into job satisfaction.

What if none of the techniques suggested so far seem to apply to you? What if you're in a job you really find boring, and you honestly don't think there's anything interesting to be learned there?

Make a game out of it: keep a notebook, and jot down something that you've learned, every day. Some information you pick up may seem so insignificant that you'd hardly think of it as "learning." Don't be too eager to dismiss it, though. Any kind of learning is rewarding, and you're looking for ways to put satisfaction into your workday, not just for skills to help you succeed.

Learn from the other people in your office. Learn from the suppliers, salespeople, and reps who come around. Find out what their jobs require of them. Ask them about their work, the products they're selling, the satisfactions they find in their own work. Learn about people's families and friends, their home lives, and their hobbies. Interview the world.

Lots of people have a second business on the side, and know how to obtain an incredible array of goods and services. Learn about these things, and become a small-scale information broker. See whether you can put a coworker in contact with a friend in ways that are mutually beneficial.

Learn about the inner workings of your own company. How does it work as a business? Where does the profit come from? What do the other departments do? What are your boss' major problems? What does your company do better (or worse) than its competitors? You can read trade publications to find out more about the other companies in the field.

Everything you learn will give you "learning satisfaction." But much of what you learn may also turn out to be useful, suggesting new possibilities which may very well lead to new successes and more interesting work.

## LEARNING OUTSIDE THE JOB

You can also learn outside the job, picking up information that will make the job itself more interesting, and adding satisfaction to your life as a whole.

● Vocational Courses:

The training your company will pay for is likely to be the kind that will enhance the skills you already have, and make you into more of what you are already. But what if you want an entirely new set of skills, because you'd like to change your line of work?

— What vocational courses are available?

— Is there a technical school nearby? Do they offer evening or weekend classes? Is there a university or college that offers extension classes?

— Are you eligible for student loans or government benefits?

— Are there any local groups that meet informally to discuss subjects that might interest you?

The information desk at your public library is probably the best place to start looking for the answers to these questions. A second approach is to call your local high school and ask for information about adult education in your school district. Many people have found a far wider range of training and intellectual excitement available in their community than they had any idea existed.

• Volunteer Learning Off-the-Job:

You can also volunteer outside your company, and receive training in a variety of areas ranging from cardiopulmonary resuscitation to counseling. All sorts of places need volunteers: charities, museums, public interest groups, or even your child's classroom. If you realize, for instance, that you will need experience in counseling to do the work that means the most to you, volunteering to serve on a crisis hotline is one way to acquire both training and experience.

— Can you obtain skills that would supplement your present abilities by volunteering outside the workplace?

• Learning by Teaching:

Kim was promoted from a secretarial job to a publicity position without having been fully trained for it. She knew she had a lot to learn, and her way of going about it was to use one of the most time-honored learning techniques: teaching what you want to learn. When she was invited to give a marketing course for her local university's extension program, she decided to make her opportunity to teach a chance to learn, too.

— Preparing her lectures forced Kim to review what she already knew about the subject, and to research areas of marketing that she was less familiar with.

— The questions her students asked helped her to clarify her understanding.

— Teaching gave her an opportunity to invite guest lecturers to speak at her classes. These professionals not only had a great deal to offer her students, they were also excellent contacts for her.

- Life Experience:

Life can teach you: but no one can possibly tell you exactly how or when. It's a surprising process, and that means it can't be predicted or forced. When you're simply going about your everyday life, even if you're temporarily out of the workforce, you can be learning—and some of what you learn, as well as some of your enthusiasm, is bound to rub off.

## DIRECTIONS TO STRETCH IN

Choosing which areas to target, in order to learn more, can be an art in itself. It is best to structure your learning so that you take advantage of your existing abilities and interests, and build skills that are adjacent to them. You might call this approach "crabwise learning," since it involves moving sideways from areas that are already familiar.

Thus a secretary might go by crabwise learning from typing

to word processing, from word processing to familiarity with the computer, and from there learn how to use the computer's spread sheets and into bookkeeping.

A facility for imitating voices can, by crabwise learning, turn into a skill as a stand-up comedian, which can evolve into radio drama, and radio drama into play or even screenplay writing. Jonathan took his ability to wisecrack with his repertoire of "funny voices," and turned it into the business of writing and producing humorous commercial spots for clients who wanted radio advertising.

If you have a green thumb, crabwise learning might lead you to find out about the basic dozen or so plants that are used in commercial settings, and so to a job with a company that leases and maintains the greenery in large office buildings. From being one of the people who makes house calls at offices to water, dust, trim, and fertilize the plants, a further crabwise step might take you to the point where you work at the plant company's showroom. You might wind up advising businesses as to the types of plants that best fit their space, lighting, and budget. Along the way you might discover that you had virtually become a salesperson, something you would originally never have expected to enjoy.

Scale modelling (airplanes) can be developed into scale modelling (architectural) by this kind of crabwise learning.

These examples may seem individualistic and quite irrelevant to your own circumstances, but there's a point behind the eclectic choice of examples. The very skills and abilities that you might never think of in terms of work potential may be the very ones that can be developed into a job peculiarly suited to your nature and temperament.

One young grandmother found that she'd become the clearinghouse for her grandchildren's clothing, as various children grew out of things and they were passed around the family. In the process of running church sales, she developed both experience and contacts in selling clothes. By crabwise building, she has connected these various skills, and has now opened her own shop which recycles children's clothes.

Crabwise learning is a technique to help you break out of a narrow area of job possibilities and build a range of available skills that work well together. As a result, your skills will qualify you for more positions, and it will become easier for you to find work that satisfies you in other ways; working for a higher wage, with people you like, or on a schedule that is more suited to your taste.

Crabwise learning builds on your areas of strength, but it is also important to balance out your strengths by working on the weaker areas. In Chapter Four, on page 75, you examined the various areas of expertise into which the workplace can be divided. We'd like you to go back to your notes on that section, choose an area in which you are weak, and go to work on it. Set yourself a goal of strengthening your skills in that area, whether by going to night classes or seminars, or by reading books, or simply by making it your business to watch people who are stronger than you in that area.

You will find yourself becoming a more balanced, more flexible human being. And you may find that your growing skills have singled you out for advancement, or have prepared you for work in areas that were previously closed to you. Making the most of what comes naturally is an important part of learning, but you can also learn to do what used to seem frankly impossible.

More important, learning can bring you closer to your optimal work, the work that suits you, and allows you to best make a contribution.

# THE INSIDE JOB

**Relevance:** Particularly important for those who would like to see their values more fully expressed in the context of their work.

**Premise:** Individuals who express their values in the workplace can have an impact on everyone around them.

**Strategy:** Work simultaneously at your "outside" job —the job for which you are paid—and at an "inside job," dictated by your values and beliefs.

**Tactics:** Work for the Job Company; give yourself a "statement of purpose;" develop overall goals, target areas and strategies for working an inside job; develop an "inside job description" that expresses the values you wish to incorporate in your work.

# Chapter 9

## THE INSIDE JOB

*I am like a spy in a higher service.*
*Soren Kierkegaard*

Many people feel as though they are crammed into their jobs like kids into last year's sneakers. The jobs are too small, too ratty, and they pinch. Soon enough, something has to give: either the sneakers or the feet themselves, either the jobs or the people. Too often, it's the person who pays the price, who keeps working at a job that no longer fits them.

Humans are often "larger" than their job descriptions, and one way to deal with a job description that "pinches" is to give yourself a private or "personal" job description that fits you better than the official one. We have explored two ways to do this already: by adding a component of "zenning it" to the work you do, and by adding an element of learning. Each of them offers you an opportunity to turn even routine work into an arena for growth and discovery, because each of them encourages you to construct a more satisfying "job-within-a-job."

This is a strategy that many people consciously or unconsciously adopt, and one which can bring real rewards in terms of work satisfaction. This chapter will look at the idea of the job-within-a-job in more detail, and offer you some additional ways to turn a less-than-meaningful job into an opportunity. These suggestions demand creativity and a sense of playfulness on your part, and are presented in the form of an extended metaphor: the Job Company.

- Karasses and Granfaloons:

Readers of Kurt Vonnegut's science fiction novel, *Cat's Cradle*, take a gleeful delight in the personality and wisdom of the book's imaginary prophet, Bokonon. Bokonon is portrayed as a calypso-singing character who creates a highly unusual religion for the natives of a fictitious South American dictatorship, the Republic of San Lorenzo. As part of this religion, he teaches them two new ideas: the concepts of the Karass and the Granfaloon.

Bokononists believe "that humanity is organized into teams, teams that do God's Will without ever discovering what they are doing." Such teams are termed karasses by Bokonon, who notes that "if you find your life tangled up with somebody else's life for no very logical reasons, that person may be a member of your karass." Consider the way in which, during periods of growth and change, new friends swim into your orbit who seem to be growing and changing along with you. There is an uncanny feeling of rightness to these friendships, which may in their turn dissolve, to be followed by others that are more appropriate to the next challenge, task, or lesson that life presents.

By contrast with karasses, Bokonon tells us, "granfaloons" are the teams that people frequently identify with, and which are "meaningless in terms of the way God gets things done." Examples of granfaloons, according to Bokonon, are "the Communist Party, the Daughters of the American Revolution, the General Electric Company, the International Order of Odd Fellows—and any nation, anytime, anywhere."

Part of the pleasure of Vonnegut's book comes from the reader's sense that Bokonon's comments on human behavior have a real basis in the ways that people actually go about the business of joining societies and groups. Granfaloons and karasses do indeed exist.

As social creatures, people enjoy the sense of "belonging" to a club, coterie, or klatch of one kind or another. Yet the fact is that the sort of associations most people join, with their definable memberships and annual dues, are more frequently granfaloons than true karasses.

As a means of exploring the implications of working at a job-within-a-job, you might wish to consider yourself a member of a karass which we have termed "The Job Company." Like Bokonon's religion, the Job Company is a purely imaginary entity. Job Company members pay no annual dues, receive no newsletters, and possess no membership cards. Yet the Job Company does in some sense exist, and being consciously employed by the Company is tantamount to having the kind of satisfying work discussed throughout this book.

## WHAT IS THE JOB COMPANY?

It is not easy to define the Job Company. Perhaps the best way is to describe it as a companionship, a loose network of the like-minded. Nikos Kazantzakis, the Greek novelist and author of *Zorba the Greek,* phrased this sense of companionship poetically: "I strive to discover how to signal my companions, to say in time a simple word, a password, like conspirators: Let us unite, let us hold each other tightly, let us merge our hearts, let us create for Earth a brain and a heart, let us give a human meaning to the superhuman struggle."

The Job Company is a companionship that is directly involved with specific issues and questions relating to work. Theodore Roszak, author of *Where the Wasteland Ends,* was speaking for many present-day members of the Company when he wrote, "In our time a secret manifesto is being written. Its language is a longing we read in one another's eyes. It is the longing to know our authentic vocation in the world, to find the work and the way of being that belongs to each of us."

Even more specifically, some (though by no means all) members of the Job Company feel that they carry within themselves some spark or memory of a higher order of reality. Kierkegaard expressed this feeling, and his sense of working "undercover" for the Company, in his phrase "I am like a spy in a higher service."

You can imagine the Company, then, as a loose association of individuals who are concerned that their work should not only feed, clothe, and interest them, but also benefit the world they live in. You could also think of it as the influence of a higher intelligence in the employment and growth of humans. It is in this second sense that one can speak of the Company providing work for us, or of dedicating one's life to the Company.

You may think the whole idea of the Company is a bit far-fetched, or it may be compatible with your own sense of hidden forces or a divine hand working in the world and in your life. It is not the business of this book to persuade you to adopt a particular view of reality. But it is our business to show you that the idea of the Company, at least on an imaginative basis, offers some profound benefits.

In the spirit of Bokonon, let us propose that a consortium of invisible forces has formed a fictitious employment agency known as the Job Company. In earlier times, these invisible forces might have been described as "angels"—but feathered creatures of this sort are a little hard to swallow nowadays, and it would be just fine if you preferred to think of them as "imaginary entities," "higher intelligences," or "natural forces at work in the development of human culture." However you conceive of them, if you are looking for work in the hard-core real world, you might seriously consider giving the Job Company a call.

*From a Job Company Prospectus:*

We are not listed in the Yellow Pages. We are as close to you as your own imagination, your values, and your sense of purpose. We are a job placement agency, specializing in undercover work. We have a vacancy for you, and we think you will agree that working for us offers you more than the usual level of job satisfaction.

The Job Company is an undercover agency. Most positions with the Company demand that your cover work be performed to higher standards than similar work done by non-Company personnel; and the work you do for the Company itself will need to be impeccable. The Company's bottom line is human excellence. But you will have all the charisma, right stuff, baraka, luck, grace, and serendipity the Company's technical team can back you up with: when you work for the Company, great things are possible.

Your work for the Job Company, for example, may require you to offer your services to an architectural firm as a draftsman. That would be your cover. Your paycheck would be cut by your cover employer's bookkeeper. You would tell your friends, proudly, sadly, or indifferently, that you work for Browne and Browne. But in reality you would be a Job Company agent, working to Job Company standards and receiving Job Company perks. The Job Company wants you to accomplish something in that architectural office that your cover boss may know nothing about, and might or might not want to pay you for if he did.

The Job Company is neither interested in your boss making a bundle on a new housing development, nor in his losing his shirt as a result of politicking in the city planning department. The Job Company may have slipped you into your architect's office either because it wants to see a particular housing project come together—which may involve utility or beauty—or for reasons utterly unconcerned with architecture.

To the casual eye, you may appear to be just a minor employee, someone who is not in a position to influence anything. Circumstances do not bear that out. The Job Company understands, and influences, how events actually work. It frequently "moves in mysterious ways" to accomplish its purposes. The idea someone else overhears you tossing out may be just that, tossed out. But it may also spark a train of thought that manages to meet the developer's budget and still increase the living space of the housing units by 15 percent.

It is safest to assume that every time you receive a placement from the Job Company, it is your human qualities that count. The Job Company may frankly not care a green fig about your drafting skills. Sure, you'll be doing your drafting, but the Company may want you there simply because it figures you have the right chemistry for the personnel mix in that office. Perhaps you have a knack for defusing explosive situations and personalities. One draftsperson may be the missing human ingredient that makes the rest of the team mesh.

But you will also have to produce, or blow your assignment. You can't just pretend to be the employee your boss is paying you to be. If you just sit around the office smiling and offering compassionate advice to everyone who walks by, neither your employer nor the Company will want to keep you in that office very long.

● Job Company Benefits:

Those who can adopt the idea of working for the Company have much to gain from it.

— Purpose: your job expresses your deeper values, not simply the requirements of the marketplace.

— Commitment: this purpose gives a sense of commitment to your work, which is seen as an opportunity to be of service. As a result, you find yourself more dedicated.

— Companionship: it offers a sense of companionship with your fellow Company workers; those who share similar values, and attempt to integrate them into their work.

— Opportunity: Job Company employees are more likely than others to take advantage of opportunities, because they are aware that the Company may be leading them in directions they would not otherwise explore. When opportunities or synchronicities present themselves, Job Company employees may feel encouraged by the sense that they are on the right track, and experience an added confidence.

All these can be considered as "not-on-the-books" benefits which the Company offers its employees. They can add up to a whole lot more than a seat in the executive dining room. And although the way the Company rewards its employees is largely invisible, it is no less real for that.

The Job Company is offered you as an hypothesis. You are encouraged to test it.

## UNDERCOVER WORK FOR THE COMPANY

The techniques in the rest of this chapter are based on the idea that even if your everyday job description has little or nothing to do with your sense of real work or vocation, your presence on the job may. We're suggesting the possibility of consciously working two jobs at the same time; one which satisfies your boss (for which you are paid) and one which pleases you (which your boss may know next to nothing about).

In this sense, you'll be working "undercover" for the Job Company. You'll be doing your "cover" job in accordance with its "official" job description, while getting satisfaction from the simultaneous performance of your "inside job": the job you do for yourself, for those whose values you share, for the Company.

We are talking about believing in yourself, and actively bringing your values, your love, and your creativity to bear at your place of work—especially if your work doesn't presently offer you a high level of satisfaction.

## DISCOVERING YOUR INSIDE JOB

The way to discover the appropriate inside job for you is to find out exactly what it is that you want to put into, and get out of, your life. Your inside job needs to include a purpose that you can work toward, attain success at, and take pride in. Think back over what you learned in chapters four and five, and write down some of the things you would like to accomplish at work. You are, in effect, defining your "statement of purpose."

You might write, "I want the work I do to reflect creativity and compassion. I intend to bring these values into my work by being more freely inventive in the way I deal with problems, and by giving a greater degree of attention to the people (rather than 'clients') who come into my office."

Or you might say, "On its tough days, life is tough enough for most people, and doesn't need to be any tougher. My purpose is simply to help out where I can." This would cover anything from leaving your house twenty minutes early to pick up a coworker, to bringing some donuts into the office.

Again, you might describe your purpose like this: "To persuade the management of the restaurant where I work to set up a no-smoking section for patrons; to include American Heart Association-approved items on the menu; and to start a staff softball team."

You will probably find yourself writing down some items that describe overall goals, some that detail specific target areas, and some which set down precise strategies. Next, you should briefly list the items in your statement of purpose in these three categories:

1. Overall Goals. Under this heading you would list general objectives, such as "to reflect creativity and compassion," "to help out where I can," or "to increase health awareness in this restaurant."

2. Target Areas. In this category you would note more specific areas that you want to work on, such as "problem-solving," "relationship with clients," "no-smoking section," "Heart Association items," and "softball team."

3. Strategies. Here you would list precise strategies for accomplishing your overall goals and targets. Examples might include "suggest creative problem-solving team to Bill," "talk to patrons about their feelings about no-smoking section," "discuss softball team with restaurant manager."

It's worth distinguishing these three levels, and identifying what your purpose looks like at each level, because getting things clear at the first level will often suggest a variety of approaches that you could take at the second and third levels. Vague, general goals and targets become realities only when they can be translated into precise strategies.

Sometimes you'll find you have an overall goal that can't be translated into target areas and specific strategies in advance. For example, the important thing about the goal of "helping out where you can" is that it is spontaneous. It can't be planned in advance since it involves responding to the actual problems and situations that arise from day to day. But in general, you'll find that most of the items you wrote down in your initial statement of purpose fall into one of the three categories.

• Inside Job Description:

When you have written your statement of purpose and broken it down into the three levels, you may find it helpful to give yourself an "inside job description" (describing what you feel your job—and your life—is "really about") which is more in line with your individuality and your ideals than with your official job description. You will find it valuable to write out your inside job description, using the format in Chapter Five, page 92.

Your inside job description details the work you do for the Job Company. Your cover job description defines the work you do for your boss.

Your inside job description might simply be "roving trouble-shooter," and your work for the Job Company would simply be to keep an eye out for situations where you can help others. But some inside job descriptions involve all three levels.

Your statement of purpose might be "to support my favorite charity," while your inside job description might read, "consultant for charitable affairs." Your target area might be to set up a canned goods drive before Thanksgiving. This would involve a number of specific strategies, such as discussing the idea with management, contacting local community organizations to find out about their needs, sending out a memo to your coworkers to solicit their assistance, coordinating colleagues with pickup trucks or vans to deliver the goods, and actually gathering the food and delivering it to the sponsoring organization.

Simply giving yourself an inside job description can make a great difference in the way you feel about your work. If you identified yourself as someone with a "slipped vocation," or one who has an archetypal role of the kind described in Chapter Five, just naming your archetypal vocation may give you enough of a hint to revolutionize your attitude toward work.

If, for example, you identified with the role of court jester, that might be your inside job title. Your cover job title might be "management consultant," and your cover work might be to introduce new management techniques. Your role as a jester, however, would involve using humor as a strategy to encourage managers to be more flexible, while giving employees increased participation.

If you discovered your inside job title independently of writing your statement of purpose, it will be helpful to translate your job description into the three levels discussed above. Specifically articulating your intentions will give you an added sense of their importance, and increase their chances of becoming a reality.

## SOME INSIDE JOB POSSIBILITIES

The rest of this chapter describes a number of possible inside jobs. The suggestions range from some that your boss would probably be delighted with, to some that he or she might be completely indifferent to. We shall end with the story of a man who worked under the Nazi regime, and managed to accomplish some goals that his boss would hardly have appreciated.

• Inside Job #1: Caring in the Workplace

Your overall goal may be as basic as improving the human interactions at your place of work. One way of exerting this kind of influence is simply to make it your business to care about the people you work with, and this could be your target area.

The strategies you'd use in this case would be of the un-planned, spontaneous sort: the kind word, the willingness to listen for a moment, the patience, humor, or helping hand with a detail that can make all the difference in someone's day.

This kind of concern for others is not an assignment from your boss, nor is it just a matter of politeness. Something happens when your politeness goes beyond a critical point. Differences in quantity can add up to very profound shifts in quality. Your concern needs to grow out of your own genuine caring.

You're working for the Job Company.

• Inside Job #2: Acting as a Catalyst

Another function you can serve is to be a catalyst, and that could be your inside job title. Your overall goal would be to encourage creative ideas. Your strategy might be simply to take a lunch break with a friend and listen to their work problems.

To enable someone's anger and frustration to express itself, and then to steer it in the direction of a solution can not only relieve the immediate distress, but also lead to positive changes.

As a catalyst, you can help others to bring their ideas out into the open, or you can use yourself as a one-person task force, and make it your business to champion the best ideas that come your way.

Many creative people can do anything but sell their own ideas to others. Perhaps you will be the one who drops a hint to the right person at the right time, and sets a project in motion that would never have got off the ground without you.

### ● Inside Job #3: Inside Perspective

Simple as it sounds, viewing your work from a different perspective can, all by itself, alter your work experience. As Morty Lefkoe of New York University's division of career and professional development points out, for employees to "redefine their jobs and then adopt new job contexts is not just an exercise in semantics. A real transformation can take place. . . ."

Joyce is a fine and sensitive horsewoman. She enjoys working with horses, and in many ways her work at the local stable is ideal. But one aspect of her job that has always bored and irritated her is raking the sand in the ring before a dressage show.

Showhorses perform intricate, almost balletic movements in the course of dressage, and unevenness in the sand can cause problems. So raking the sand carefully and thoroughly before the show is an important task. It lacks one ingredient, however, that makes the rest of Joyce's work so enjoyable: it doesn't involve any direct contact with horses.

Joyce considered this task real drudge work until one day she read about the famous sand gardens in Japanese zen monasteries. After that, she began to rake the arena "as if" she was a monk at Daitokuji. She poured herself into the task with a care and attention that she'd never felt before, raking the sand with quiet, meditative joy.

She'd not only given herself an inside job title, "zen gardener," she'd given herself a different focus, and discovered her own version of zenning it in the process.

● Inside Job #4: Inside Charity

We have been suggesting personal things you might choose as part of your hidden agenda. But what if self-discovery and the one-to-one communication we have been discussing seem too limited in scope?

Jurgen decided to set up a blood drive for the Red Cross at the company where he works. He circulated a sign-up sheet around the plant to gather volunteer blood donors, and arranged with the management to give each person an hour off work (with pay) while they gave blood and rested. The Red Cross scheduled a day when the bloodmobile could come. And the result? A company that employs around 200 people provided about 40 pints of blood.

There are many ways to make a charity your special project while you go about your job. Discover what your company's policies on charitable donations are. Most large corporations have an allowance in their annual budget for donations to non-profit organizations, and many of them are willing—even eager —to match any funds their employees contribute up to a dollar limit per employee. Find out who else in the office is interested in the issues that concern you. Do some fundraising. Get on the committee that distributes the funds. Or take matters even further into your own hands, like Jurgen, and set up an event which will support the charity of your choice.

Albert Einstein did some of this kind of "charitable underwriting," too. When his Theory of Relativity was finally vindicated by British scientists in 1919, Einstein became famous overnight. Reporters arrived all day in a continual stream to interview him, and no free photos were available. Instead, Einstein sold the reporters his portrait, and dedicated the proceeds to the starving children of Vienna.

● Inside Job #5: Values Education

Paul Katzeff is chairman of the Specialty Coffee Roasters Association. During the turbulent sixties, he worked with street gangs on the Lower East Side of New York after earning his master's degree in social work. He got into the food business by organizing food-buying groups in East Harlem, as a way to talk to the parents of gang members. "I found that if I could save parents 50 percent on their groceries, they'd listen," he said.

After a while Katzeff experienced "helper's burnout," and relocated to get his own life in order. In 1971 Katzeff began his own company, roasting specialty coffees for the gourmet food trade. At the time there were only four companies of this type in the country, but the market grew rapidly.

When he became chairman of the Association, Katzeff once again turned his attention to values, this time by inviting speakers who were knowledgeable about Central America to address the members and retailers at the association's biannual convention.

Paul Katzeff is an independent entrepreneur, and educating his colleagues about which countries have profit sharing for plantation workers is hardly something that the job demands. But it means something to him, and he did something about it. There is, as they say, more than one bottom line.

There are many ways in which you can take the values you hold and apply them in your work. You can influence other people or you can influence company policy. The important thing is to put your values to work. You can sometimes bring about profound change by starting in a very small way. Two working mothers talking about on-site day-care facilities for their children can be the beginning of important change.

If you're in a large corporate situation, you may not be able to affect the entire corporation. But if you can influence the ten workstations around you, you have no way of telling how far the effect might spread. It might extend to the whole plant, the district, the division, and, eventually, the entire corporation.

As Thomas Peters points out in *Passion for Excellence,* if you "commit yourself to performing one ten-minute act of exceptional customer courtesy per day," and induce your colleagues in a 100-person company to do the same, "taking into account normal vacations, holidays, etc., that would mean 24,000 new courteous acts per year. Such is the stuff of revolutions!"

Even if your accomplishments affect relatively few people, you will have succeeded in putting your values to work, and you can take pride in that.

Not every boss is going to be receptive, of course, and not every company will be willing to help you. If you discover your company is unwilling to reflect your values in any way, shape, or form, you've realized something very important about your place of work. Perhaps you'll want to seriously consider shifting to a different company.

## THE QUINTESSENTIAL INSIDE JOB

As a reminder that it is possible to work with humanity and love in the most unexpected of circumstances, we would like to introduce to you a man named Oskar Schindler; a man who served a humanistic purpose in the heart of the Nazi regime in Poland. His story has been marvelously documented by the Australian writer Thomas Kenneally, in his award-winning novel, *Schindler's List.*

Oskar Schindler is a fairly unique example of someone whose "inside" job description would have been totally unacceptable to his bosses.

Schindler was a German industrialist, a man fond of drinking and women, and acquainted with a number of high-ranking Nazi officers, including Commandant Goeth of the forced labor camp, Plaszow. Not that Schindler listed Goeth among his friends. But the commandant was a man who served his purposes, a man to be wined and dined.

Schindler's true purpose was to save the lives of Jews who would otherwise wind up in Auschwitz. He went about it in a most remarkable way. Taking advantage of the extremely cheap labor available from Jews in the forced labor camps, he bribed, charmed, and finagled his way into building an SS forced labor subcamp at his own cost, inside the grounds of his own factory.

When the Germans wished to send "Schindler's Jews" to Auschwitz, there would always be a problem. Schindler said that he was making armaments for the German war effort, and couldn't spare those particular people; although the fact is that no armaments were ever actually delivered to the German troops from Schindler's factory.

When three hundred of his women workers were finally transferred against his wishes to Auschwitz, Schindler sent a pretty girl with a bribe of ham, liquor, and diamonds to persuade the commandant to send them back. He followed this up by arranging for another 3,000 women to be shipped out from Auschwitz to other small factory camps in Moravia.

Schindler promised the Jews who worked for him very early on during the German occupation of Poland that they would survive the the war. And they did. As an international Jewish relief organization later stated, "Schindler's camp in Brinnlitz was the only camp in the Nazi-occupied territories where a Jew was never killed, or even beaten, but was always treated as a human being."

It is sometimes possible to work great good in unlikely circumstances.

# THE INSIDE JOB YOU NEVER KNEW YOU WERE DOING

So far, we have talked about the ways in which you can deliberately set out to integrate your values into your work. But there are other ways to get things accomplished besides developing goals and carrying them out.

● The Human Presence:

John Rassias, a professor at Dartmouth and a distinguished teacher of Romance languages, recounts an incident which took place early in his career as an academic when he served on a joint student-faculty committee.

One of their meetings was in progress when a student member appeared at the door of the room where the committee was in session. The student looked in through the open door and saw faculty faces looking impatient ("how like the students to be late") and his fellow students looking, if possible, even more disgruntled ("he's letting us down").

The student did five or six chin-ups on the doorframe, as if to express his dismay at the whole affair, at which point Rassias bounded to his feet, came over to the door, and told the astonished student, "I like that. I like a man who has the guts to express his feelings." Then Rassias proceeded to push the student aside and try some chin-ups himself. When he'd made a reasonably successful showing, he put his arm round the student's shoulders and escorted him into the meeting.

For John Rassias, it was probably just another incident in yet another committee meeting. But the student remembered. Years later he ran into Rassias, and told him what had been going through his mind that day.

"I'd decided to kill myself," he said. "I felt that human beings just weren't up to much, and I was ready to throw in the towel. I told myself I'd go to the committee meeting and give people one last chance to show they had any heart or soul. And when I looked into that room and saw those faces, with even my fellow students looking annoyed at me, I had my answer. People just weren't worth staying alive for. And then you came to the door. I just want to let you know that I'm alive because of what you did that day."

Cast your mind back over the last few years and recall those occasions when someone made a casual remark that gave you a new direction in your life. The most important ideas and discoveries are sometimes triggered by a chance remark from someone who has no idea of the impact their words will have.

It's worth remembering that even if you never use any of the techniques we have suggested in this chapter, your presence and the human values you embody are likely to change things.

Perhaps more often than we think, the jobs we underrate at the time have an important impact on the lives of those around us. They can also contribute skills and contacts that become unexpectedly important to us later on.

A rising songwriter of our acquaintance worked for a while in a "boiler room," one of those telephone sales operations that encourage consumers to buy a product they may not really want. Duncan didn't stay in the boiler room for long, but even a season in hell can have its advantages. In retrospect, Duncan's time in the boiler room did have important side effects. It taught him a great deal about making his goals clear and about marketing. Today he is more creative, and far more persistent, about getting his material heard by the right people.

Any job, no matter how little you think of it, may include elements that will be of great significance in your later development, or in the growth of those around you. You may be doing an inside job that you do not recognize as such, either by picking up skills and contacts that will prove useful later on, or simply by touching people deeply in ways that you are unaware of.

## THE SUBTLE NATIONAL PRODUCT

This chapter has introduced a number of notions designed to put the spotlight on the second and third levels of satisfaction. We would like to conclude with one last idea. Economists currently evaluate the work of a nation in terms of its Gross National Product or GNP, which is defined as that nation's "total output of goods and services" in a year. We would like to propose that a Subtle National Product must also exist.

The Subtle National Product would be defined as a given nation's contribution to the real betterment of life on this planet in the course of a year. This would naturally include actions to resolve political conflicts, avoid warfare, and improve the environment. But it would also include: the quality of care and attention that a teacher brings to his students; or a physician to her patients; the love that goes into the preparation of food; and the creativity and inspiration of the artist.

Whatever you may think of the Job Company, the Subtle National Product certainly does exist, and the reason most economists largely ignore it is because it is qualitative rather than quantitative. It cannot be measured. But it is no less real for that.

Most of us receive our paychecks for the contributions we make to the Gross National Product. It is our contribution to the Subtle National Product, though, that makes us human, and our work for the Job Company that gives us the warmest satisfaction.

# Chapter 13

# OPTIMAL WORK

**Relevance:**    We all want our work to be optimal.

**Premise:**    Shooting for the top includes shooting for top-level fulfillment.

**Strategy:**    Do the work you dream of, and get paid for it.

**Tactics:**    Discover your dream; fine tune your present job; make a major change; take courage from the examples of people like Picasso and Einstein; reach the breakthrough point.

# Chapter 10

# OPTIMAL WORK

*Where one's work is concerned, one should be an
epicure.*

Eugene Delacroix

There's an Italian gambler's proverb that says "The wheel is
crooked, but people have been known to win." Life is a little like
roulette, and not everyone winds up with work that fits them
precisely. Yet we are all looking for the ideal situation, the
perfect job, the work that gives us total satisfaction with no
drawbacks.

What would the perfect job look like, if it did exist?

It would presumably be the kind of work which paid more
than you knew how to spend, involved no drudgery, and made
a terrific contribution to the world around you. It would be a
place where the people you worked with were always friendly
and where nobody minded if you came in late. President of the
U.S. in a world at peace, with Woody Allen as an advisor in your
kitchen cabinet, perhaps.

Nice work if you can get it, but you can't. People being
people, and work being work, this kind of perfection clearly
doesn't exist. This chapter deals with optimal work, not perfect
work. The difference is crucial: it's the difference between a pipe
dream and a reality. Optimal work means work that's optimal in
real-world terms.

Optimal work, then, is likely to be the kind that pays you a good wage, suits your personality, your skills and your values, involves a minimal amount of drudgery, and makes some kind of real contribution. It's a job where you like the people you work with, where there is enough excitement to keep you interested, and not so much stress that you end up a basket case. That kind of work does exist, and finding it is one of the most worthwhile things you could ever do.

This book has offered a number of guidelines for you to consider in choosing or evaluating your work. It has also emphasized the importance of second and third level satisfactions. But these are just suggestions, and they are only as relevant to your situation as you find them to be. There are two sides to optimal work, and the rest of this chapter explores them.

## FINDING THE OPTIMAL JOB

Optimal work is work that, for all its limitations, is excellently suited to your present situation, needs, and abilities. Every person's optimal work will be something uniquely suited to them. No guidelines can cover it, no strategies can guarantee it, and no definition can quite capture it except the definition that runs: "If you feel it's optimal, it is."

When asked to sum up her advice to the students she counsels, Susan Zurcher, a placement counselor at Indiana State University, said, "I basically counsel people to follow their own hearts."

It is a commonplace of psychology that we all tend to internalize the values and opinions of people whom we respect. Indeed, if we didn't, we'd have very little notion of our own values and opinions. But many of us hold the ideas we picked up from others as though they were our own, and the result is that we work toward dreams and ambitions that are not rooted in our own nature.

Finding optimal work involves finding one's own values, interests, and abilities. It is a matter of contacting one's personal sense of purpose, and it cannot be accomplished while "what other people will think" weighs more heavily on us than how we feel.

Obtaining optimal work requires knowing one's own self as well as one's skills and the marketplace. The things you delight in, the parts of your job that bring you alive, that stimulate your curiosity, your creativity, or your ability to give of yourself, your interests, fascinations, and passions: these are what count as you search for truly optimal work. These are not things you can borrow from other people, no matter how much you may admire them. They have to grow in your own soil and soul.

Perhaps, in the course of this book, you have come to recognize your optimal job. You have located your dream; it satisfies the criteria for optimal work; and all that remains is for you to trust in yourself and hit the road. You may need to work your way up to your optimal job, or underwrite it for a while; but you know what it looks like, and with determination you can move toward it.

Barbara Sher, in her fine book, *Wishcraft: How to Get What You Really Want,* makes a somewhat astounding statement. "I don't care what you've accomplished in your life or what your IQ is," she writes, "you were born with your own unique kind of genius. And I mean that in the fullest sense of the word. Not genius with a small 'g' as opposed to Albert Einstein. Big 'G' genius, like Albert Einstein."

Perhaps that's an overstatement, and perhaps it isn't. Barbara Sher certainly makes a strong case for it. She argues that the brilliance, vision, and determination that we recognize in those we call geniuses are present in everyone at an early age. She suggests they account for your ability to pick up a language or two in the first four years of life, speaking them with a fluency that you would be hard pressed to achieve by living five adult years in a foreign country. Whether or not you feel that everyone is born with an Einstein level of genius, you must admit that if you could continue to maintain the rate of learning you managed as a child, you wouldn't be far short of brilliant.

Indeed, many people of genius regard their talents as the result of a capacity to retain the infectious enthusiasm of childhood. The Swedish filmmaker Ingmar Bergman put it this way: "All of us collect fortunes when we are children—a fortune of colors, of lights and darkness, of movements, of tensions. Some of us have the fantastic chance to go back to our fortune when we grow up." The American poet William Stafford declares that he's always puzzled when people ask him why he writes poetry. "For me the puzzle is not that some people are still writing," he says, "the real question is why did the other people stop."

A biographer describes Albert Schweitzer thus: "he existed in the confident, indisputable way that animals and children exist, his concentration at every moment completely focused on whoever or whatever then occupied his mind." This childlike pouring of oneself into the moment is the essence of what we have called "zenning it," but it is also of the essence of real love.

As you set out to find your optimal work, learn to trust yourself. Trust in your own genius. If you feel you need to think of it in terms of a small "g," that's fine. If you'd like to shoot for the big "G," that's even better. But stretch your trust in yourself and your innate capacities. Remember that every job you might envy is a job that someone has managed to get; someone who trusted themselves enough to try for it.

## MOVING TOWARD OPTIMAL WORK

Moving closer to your optimal work may involve making large changes in your life, or it may only involve fine-tuning. It may require a profound change of attitude, or the simple application of common sense and creativity in a few small areas of your life.

● Finding Optimal Work Where You Least Expect It:

Have you, by any chance, already found your way into your optimal work, perhaps without even noticing? Before you answer this question, we'd like you to read on to the end of this section.

It may sound like a strange question. You might think, if I'd found my ideal job, surely I'd know it. But when we look at our lives closely, we find that we often get what we want without quite realizing we have it.

Consider the business of relationships. Have you ever been in the position where you realized that the person you live with, who frustrates you so much of the time, is actually just right for you, frustrations and all? Or think about birthday gifts. Have you ever received a piece of clothing, say, that you wouldn't have picked out for yourself, and then found that as you wore it, it "grew on you"?

Wanting something, and finding it's just right for you, are two different processes which don't always match one another. So before you go out and try to locate the work you want, perhaps you should ask yourself whether the job you already have might not be the one you're looking for.

You may have seen James Stewart in Frank Capra's classic film, *It's a Wonderful Life*. Stewart played the part of George Bailey, a man who started off with large dreams and ambitions. "I'm shaking the dust of this crummy little town off my feet and I'm gonna see the world—Italy, Greece, the Parthenon, the Coliseum—and then I'm coming back here and go to college and see what they know, and then I'm gonna build things. I'm gonna build airfields, skyscrapers a hundred stories high. I'm gonna build bridges a mile long. . . ."

Things didn't turn out quite that way for George. His father's death forced him to cancel his trip and stay behind to run the family business while his younger brother went to college and became a football star. And it got worse from there. Finally

Bailey, through no fault of his own, faces bankruptcy and scandal. His life has been one long chain of disasters, and he decides to commit suicide.

On the night he would have killed himself, however, George Bailey (with a little help from his guardian angel) is shown the world as it would have been had he never existed. He discovers the impact he has had on the lives of the people in the little town he never left, and the love that they feel toward him. He finds they have quietly come up with the money to rescue his business. By the end of the film, George has come to understand that everything that was wrong with his life had its own sort of rightness all along.

George Bailey's situation is a little extreme. After all, *It's a Wonderful Life* is a movie. But there's something about George's predicament that speaks to many of us: it's the difference between how he perceived his life, and its reality.

Like George Bailey, you may already be in the right place.

Sarah had a job running the business office of a consortium of twenty emergency room physicians. The salary was poor and the job revolved around a month-long routine. Any unforeseen events were to be dealt with smoothly, and nothing was supposed to go wrong. The up side of the situation was this: as long as Sarah took care of things flawlessly, the boss was too busy practicing medicine to drive a hundred miles from his home in another city to the office.

Sarah's boss actually only visited the office once in two years, and for the most part handled situations by phone. Sarah's job allowed her to lease an office in the location she chose, and play the kind of music she liked on the company's stereo system. The job didn't include any health plan, retirement benefits, or profit sharing, although the perks did cover purchasing a record every two weeks on the company account. The hours were "however long it takes," but Sarah could do the work at her own convenience. Many aspects of the work were perfect, and the trade-offs seemed worthwhile.

True, the job didn't offer much third-level satisfaction. It didn't even pay well. And yet Sarah came to feel that it was optimal, because she could work when she wanted to. And, every increase in efficiency meant she was able to leave work earlier. It gave Sarah time to live her own life.

If you still think your present job isn't optimal, or you feel it has served its purpose on the way to better things, read on.

● Fine Tuning:

Many optimal jobs don't start out that way, but the people who fill them can sometimes tailor them to their own personal needs and unique styles.

If your present job can be customized in this way, you will certainly want to set about customizing it. In your situation, the following will be key issues:

— increasing your emphasis on those parts of the job you like;

— maintaining a commitment to quality;

— creating pleasant human relations at the workplace; and

— increasing the degree to which your work reflects your values.

This is an area where you need to be sensitive to the opportunities chance offers you. Every business goes through changes, and those are generally the moments when things are most flexible. Whether you have just received a promotion, the business has moved to a new building, or one of the partners has been bought out, it may be your best opportunity to set something in motion that's more to your taste.

• Locating the Dream:

What if you haven't yet recognized that elusive dream?

Many women who have brought up a family, and many people who are facing a mid-life career change, know very well what their skills are—and what their work would look like, if they continued to apply those skills. But their dream is something else, and they may not even know what it is.

Locating your dream, if it has little to do with your skills and aptitudes, has to be a matter of knowing who you are in a new and different sense. It's no longer a question of identifying yourself in terms of a job description. You need to find your identity at more profound levels than those at which you have previously worked.

You'll need to set aside the sense of identity that comes with accomplishment and discover what it is that really drives you. Your task is to break out of your professional mold ("I'm a civil engineer") and to use your creativity to discover new ways of looking at yourself. If your optimal work has little to do with the skills you already have, you're bound to find some hints in some other area of your life. You need to find them.

If these questions still don't suggest anything, you might consider stronger medicine. Many Native Americans go on what they call a "vision quest" to find a sense of what their lives should contain. The quest involves spending several days alone on a hillside, fasting, and "crying for a vision." John G. Neihardt's book, *Black Elk Speaks,* contains a wonderful account of one very remarkable man's vision. Many Christians find it helpful to go on retreat for the same kind of purpose.

It might help you to set aside a weekend, or even a week's vacation time, to spend by yourself. Make sure you have no other obligations. Disconnect the phone, or take yourself camping. Spend the time probing yourself for an answer to that one question: "What would my dream job look like?"

Your optimal work for the present is to explore your dream further, and to discover your optimal job.

## COMMITMENT: THE OPTIMAL ATTITUDE

Optimal work isn't just a matter of finding the optimal job. The most essential ingredient is to have an optimal attitude to the work you do. Doing the work you love is wonderful, but loving the work you do is even more important. Remember, it's the attitude that makes the work flow.

André Soltner, the chef of New York's prestigious Lutèce restaurant, told an interviewer, "I am more than thirty years a chef. I know what I am doing and each day I do my absolute best. I cook for you from my heart, with love. It must be the same with service. The waiter must serve with love. Otherwise, the food is nothing. Do you see? Many times, I will leave my kitchen and go to the tables to take the orders myself. It starts right then and there. That feeling the customer must have is relaxation. If not, then his evening is ruined. Mine, too, by the way. How can he love, if he's not relaxed? People ask me all the time what secrets I have. I tell them there is nothing mysterious about Lutèce. I put love in my cooking and love in the serving. That is all."

Optimal work is a love affair, and successful love affairs demand a sense of responsibility and commitment. The people whose work impresses us most tend to feel not only that quality is of the essence, but that it takes a lifetime to learn what life and work are all about.

The great Japanese painter and wood engraver Hokusai lived to a fine old age, and throughout his life he was constantly learning. "I have been in love with painting ever since I became conscious of it at the age of six," he once wrote. "I drew some pictures I thought were fairly good when I was fifty, but really nothing I did before the age of seventy was of any value at all.

At seventy-three I have at last caught every aspect of nature: birds, fish, animals, insects, trees, grasses, all. When I am eighty I shall have developed still further, and I will master the secrets of art at ninety. When I reach one hundred my work will be truly sublime, and my final goal will be attained around the age of one hundred and ten, when every line and dot I draw will be imbued with life."

The philosopher W.H. Murray expressed the kind of determination that's needed for optimal work in the following paragraph:

> Until one is committed there is hesitancy, the chance to draw back, always ineffectiveness. Concerning all acts of initiative (and creation), there is one elementary truth, the ignorance of which kills countless ideas and splendid plans: that the moment one definitely commits oneself, then Providence moves too. All sorts of things occur to help one that would never otherwise have occurred. A whole stream of events issues from the decision, raising in one's favor all manner of unforseen incidents and meetings and material assistance, which no man could have dreamt would have come his way.

It almost goes without saying that people who take advantage of the opportunities that arise in their lives tend to achieve their goals more often than people who don't. However, there's another aspect to taking advantage of opportunity, and it's particularly important for people who want their work to be a learning and growing experience: "All sorts of things occur to help one."

Psychologist Carl Jung coined the term "synchronicity" to refer to meaningful chance or coincidence. Synchronicity in the world of work is what happens when the unexpected takes a hand in finding you a job, brings you the contact you've needed, or "suggests" a new avenue for you to explore.

In 1927, at the age of thirty-two, the great architect and

engineer Buckminster Fuller began to treat his life as an experiment. He set out to discover "what—if anything—a healthy young human male of average size, experience and capability with an economically dependent wife and newborn child, starting without capital or any kind of wealth, cash savings, account monies, credit, or university degree, could effectively do that could not be done by great nations or great private enterprise to lastingly improve the physical protection and support of all human lives. . . ."

Fuller believed that "the possibility of the good life for any man depends on the possibility of realizing it for all men," and he wanted to realize those possibilities. In his own words, he set out to do "what nature wanted done," and to do it in "promising ways, permitted by nature's principles." He inferred that what nature wanted done, in his case, was "the design, production, and demonstration" of artifacts which answered to major human needs that were not being met elsewhere.

This "healthy young human male" went on to popularize the principle of synergy, which is the idea that "whole systems (such as living things) behave in ways that cannot be predicted from the behaviors of their individual parts." He invented such things as the dymaxion projection, for drawing maps of a spherical world on flat paper, and the geodesic dome, one of the major architectural breakthroughs of this century.

Buckminster Fuller held decidedly unusual views on the importance of making money. "I noted that nature did not require hydrogen to 'earn a living' before allowing hydrogen to behave in the unique manner in which it does," he wrote. "Nature does not require that any of its intercompleting members 'earn a living.'" Accordingly, he worked at what seemed necessary, and trusted that what he called "nature" would support him.

He found that his financial requirements were "provided for by seemingly pure happenstance," "only coincidentally." Fuller described this coincidental support as "unbudgetable, yet realistic." In short, he attempted to align his work with the necessities of the human situation, and coincidence entered the picture.

Buckminster Fuller is one of the clearest and most extreme examples of those who feel that as long as the second and third levels of satisfaction are taken to the limit, God, nature, synchronicity, or sheer good luck will take care of first level details.

This idea of meaningful coincidence, or synchronicity, may seem relevant or irrelevant, plausible or implausible. You may accept or reject it as a philosophy. But either way, you would do well to admit that taking advantage of opportunities is a worthwhile business, and that doing what needs to be done makes sense. If synchronicity favors you, whether you call it Lady Luck or the grace of God, your open-minded attitude will have paid off.

## THE REWARDS OF OPTIMAL WORK

Those who find their optimal work characteristically describe themselves as experiencing two somewhat special ways in which their work affects them. One is the sense that at times they move into a special gear or "overdrive," and the other is that they eventually reach a breakthrough point, after which their work doesn't seem like work anymore.

• Overdrive:

Optimal work often gives people the sense that something deeper than their own individual motivations and interests are at work.

Ron, a physician, sometimes works shifts in the emergency room of a large inner-city hospital. It's a rough job as medical work goes. Often, there's very little going on, and the night shift tends to be boring. Then there are the times when victims of car crashes, knife and gunshot wounds come in. They are often close to death, and require immediate assistance of an extremely delicate sort if they are to survive.

Mostly, it's just hard, demanding work. But once or twice a year, as a guerney is being rolled in from an ambulance, Ron gets a special feeling. During these times, Ron doesn't necessarily follow the book. He may not even proceed with the immediate care procedures in the conventional order. Instead, he obeys his immediate sense of what's needed, something which others might call a hunch but which he calls "knowing." Time seems to slow down, and Ron goes to work with a calm certainty that springs from his years of experience, but also from some deeper sense of purpose. His refusal to follow the rules at times like these has saved more than one life.

Creative people will often acknowledge that there's something which dictates or inspires their creative work. It might be surprising to realize, though, that this kind of intuition also plays its part in the lives of physicians, race car drivers, and Heisman Trophy winners.

Work that involves this sort of overdrive is often the most satisfying work of all. It is almost impossible to put into words either what it feels like, or what one must do to develop this ability.

This kind of inspired involvement cannot be deliberately created, but there are certain things one can do to prepare for it. It seems to come to those who throw themselves into their work, rather than to those who "get by." It is more likely to happen to those who work for something more than money and status. It is more frequently found in children, and in those with a developed sense of play than in those who are deadly serious. And it involves, voluntarily or involuntarily, a kind of self-surrender. Further than that, one can only say that it is more like a knack than a trainable skill, and that its effects are usually wonderful.

- Breakthrough:

One of the characteristics of geniuses is their incredible fascination with their work. It's easy to see that the closer one comes to doing the work for which one feels most suited, the more fascinating and absorbing that work will seem.

There is a sense in which all the strategies and techniques that have been discussed in this book fall short of what you as a human being are capable of. Considerations of money, skill, and service to others all have their place in discovering your life's work: but there comes a time when these considerations, like the scaffolding around a building, fall away.

A time comes when you reach a breakthrough point; when enough things are going right in your world. You are delighted to be doing your work, yet like everyone else, you still face obstacles; but whereas before you tried to avoid them, they now no longer oppress you. They are part of the grist for the mill of your life, and you no longer feel the need to fight them. They are simply situations to be dealt with, no more and no less.

You have used the strategies that seemed appropriate. You have taken advantage of the opportunities that have come your way, and have tried to make your work an expression of your being. Perhaps you have suffered through some miserable circumstances, and perhaps you have tasted success. The strategies are not important to you any more. Somehow, you have reached your breakthrough point.

From now on, your satisfaction is not measured in terms of favorable or unfavorable circumstances: your work has become a natural part of being alive. Picasso expressed this feeling very clearly: "Always, you put more of yourself into your work, until one day, you never know exactly which day, it happens: you are your work." That's when, in Picasso's memorable phrase, your work becomes "the ultimate seduction."

# A PERSONAL NOTE

Norman Cousins tells a story about his friend, Pablo Casals. It is a story that has meant much to us personally, for it is the story of a life's work that was accomplished in love, and the singular way in which it was rewarded.

Pablo Casals, the great cellist, visited a friend of his, Wilhelm Kuchs, after World War II. Casals had known Kuchs as head of the Friends of Music in Vienna, and a man who had done much for music. In addition, before the war Kuchs had owned a number of historic musical instruments, Stradivarius and Guarneri violins among them, together with what may have been the world's finest collection of musical manuscripts.

When the war ended, Casals was overjoyed to hear that his friend had survived the Nazi regime and was now living in Switzerland. Casals went to pay his respects. After the two friends had embraced, Casals mentioned his concern that Kuchs' collection might have fallen into the hands of the Nazis.

Kuchs said that he had managed to save his entire collection, and began to pass Schubert and Mozart manuscripts across the table for Casals to look at. Finally, he placed on the table the manuscript of the Brahms B-flat Quartet, the piece of music which Casals loved above all others. Casals later wrote, "I suppose every musician feels that there is one piece that speaks to him alone, one which he feels seems to involve every molecule of his being. This was the way I had felt about the B-flat Quartet ever since I played it for the first time. And always I felt it was mine."

Something happened to Casals' face as he held that manuscript in his hand, and Kuchs very delicately suggested that he keep it. "It is your quartet in every way," Kuchs said, "and it would make me happy if you would let me give it to you."

Shortly thereafter Casals wrote his friend, to express something of the momentous preciousness of the gift and his appreciation of it. In return, he received a letter from Kuchs that told him some things about the writing of that quartet which he had not previously known. One fact above all struck Casals. It happens that Brahms started to write the quartet nine months before Casals' birth, and completed it on the very day Casals was born.

*****

May you find the work you were born for, and live the life you have dreamed of.